Sick in Bed,
ACROSS TWO CHAIRS,
with My Feet Out
through
the Window

GRANDPA PIKE

BOULDER
BOOKS

© 2021 Laurie Blackwood Pike

Library and Archives Canada Cataloguing in Publication

Title: Sick in bed, across two chairs, with my feet out through the window / Grandpa Pike.

Names: Grandpa Pike, 1944- author.
Identifiers: Canadiana 20210228873 | ISBN 9781989417362 (softcover)
Subjects: LCSH: Grandpa Pike, 1944-—Anecdotes. |
LCSH: Newfoundland and Labrador—Biography—
    Anecdotes. | LCSH: New Brunswick—Biography—Anecdotes. |
LCSH: Nova Scotia—Biography—Anecdotes. |
LCGFT: Anecdotes.
Classification: LCC FC2005 .G73 2021 | DDC 971.5—dc23

Published by Boulder Books
Portugal Cove-St. Philip's, Newfoundland and Labrador
www.boulderbooks.ca

Design and layout: Tanya Montini
Copy editor: Iona Bulgin
Cover design: Ashley Quirke

Printed in Canada

We acknowledge the financial support of the Government
of Newfoundland and Labrador through the
Department of Tourism, Culture, Arts and Recreation.

Funded by the
Government
of Canada

Financé par le
gouvernement
du Canada

Canada

CONTENTS

CHAPTER 3
NEWFOUNDLANDERS IN THE PROMISED LAND 41

CHAPTER 4
PEOPLE I WON'T FORGET 94

CHAPTER 5
QUIRKS, QUIPS, AND QUARE HANDS . . . 117

CHAPTER 6
ROAD WARRIOR 130

CHAPTER 7

CHAPTER 8

CHAPTER 1

THE GOOD OLD DAYS

Most of us live in the now. Living in the moment, we don't consider how much our lives will change—or how the seemingly mundane or merely interesting will become "the good old days" to us as we grow older.

"The good old days" are gone, but still with us, as our memories.

Here are a few random ones of mine, from long ago.

OF T-BIRDS
and
LOVE AFFAIRS

My affair with T-Birds didn't start in 1955—the model year of the first Thunderbird. In 1955, and through to 1965, it was all about Chevys for me. In my late teens and 20s, I knew a few people who drove a T-Bird, or Austin-Healy, or Triumph, but sports cars were mostly the province of the rich kids.

Most of the rest of us drove Chevys or Fords—cars that would hold six or eight people. The person driving the T-Bird was going with their date, or alone, to a party. The rest of us *were the party* crammed into a big car, looking for a place to make it happen.

Then I met a guy in the early 1960s who drove a white 1963 T-Bird. By then this model had grown wider, longer, and had a big back seat. We became friendly. I drove his car and I rode in it with him a few times, and I fell in love with T-Birds. He was living in Burlington, Ontario, and working at International Harvester there. He had a responsible, well-paying job. I believe he had been transferred there from Louisville, Kentucky.

I forget his name, and I lost track of him when I moved back east in 1975. What I do remember, though, was that he drove back to Kentucky every weekend to be with his girlfriend. A nine-to 10-hour drive in good summer weather. He'd leave Burlington at 5 p.m. Friday and arrive in Louisville at 4 or 5 a.m. Saturday morning, grab a few hours sleep, and spend Saturday with his girl. Sunday morning, he was back in his car to drive to Burlington. Must have been some woman, eh?

Because of him, I always wanted a 1963 T-Bird. I swore that I'd own one someday. Finally, I did, in the late 1970s!

I'd flown from Moncton to St. John's to travel with my company's sales representative there, and he picked me up in a 1963 T-Bird. I got in the passenger's seat, and said to Peter, "I want this car." Peter didn't want to sell it. By the end of the week, however, I was able to convince him. We made a deal. I cancelled my return flight and drove the car back to New Brunswick.

It was white with a black landau top, had a 390 motor, bucket seats, swing-away steering wheel, light blue leather interior, seat belts, and it went like a rocket! I called it big bird and had a stuffed toy of Big Bird on the dash.

I didn't have a garage to park it in, and we already had my company car and my wife's car in the driveway, so I didn't get to drive it a whole lot. I stored it in the winters. I took it to PEI a few years later, and Dr. Dave Dingwell's brother fell in love with it. I sold it to him. A few months after that, regret over the sale was so strong that I went back to PEI and convinced him to sell it back to me.

I kept it for a few more years, and when the company I worked for went under, I had to return their company car. I got another travelling job but needed to supply my own newer model vehicle. In a three-way trade arranged by a friend, I got a late model Chevy, he got a truck he wanted, and the third party, whom I did not meet, got the T-Bird.

Later I wanted it back. I found that it had been resold to a guy in the Woodstock, New Brunswick, area. I couldn't get his name—but whenever I was in that area, in my sales job, I'd drive around for hours at night trying to spot it. I never did. Finally, I gave up looking.

I still wonder where my baby is. I also wonder if the girlfriend of that guy I knew in Burlington, who drove his T-Bird weekly to Kentucky to see her, ever said yes to his marriage proposal. If not, why not? And if she did, do they still drive around in it on weekends? I suspect that they do. He was more persistent and determined than I am.

Kathleen Pike and Grandpa Pike on their wedding day.
"Big Bird" and Albert County Museum in the background.

GIVING
or
EXCHANGING GIFTS

I don't remember the *exchanging* part in my childhood. I remember *receiving*, from my parents—mostly clothing, often mittens or socks or something else my mother could make. The receiving was nice, especially the gifts of toys and books from Aunt Hazel in Newfoundland. In adulthood, I've never exchanged birthday or Christmas gifts with any of my brothers and sisters, only with my wife and daughter.

I still like giving gifts, although I never know what to get. But mostly it's the receiving part with which I now have trouble. I never know what to say. If I'm given something that I will never wear, I will say thank you, but I can't find words to say how wonderful it is.

To me, if you are going to give a gift, you shouldn't save it for a birthday or Christmas. Give something, now, that has meaning to you—not something you went out and bought because it is the custom to return a favour. If you give me something that you already own and love, I will treasure it forever.

Around 1973, my best friend Peter gave me his buckskin jacket. It was dark brown with a foot-long fringe on the sleeves, across the chest area, and at the bottom hem. He wore it everywhere. I admired it so much that one day as we were sitting and talking

Wally Jacket 1   Grandpa Jacket 2   Jethro Jacket 2

about a completely different subject, he got up, took it off, and handed it to me. "Here, I want you to have this," he said.

I objected. "What?" he said, in his pseudo-grumpy way. "I should give you, instead, some old worn-out thing that I don't want any more?" I accepted it and wore it for many years. A few years after I received his jacket, Peter died of a massive heart attack.

I continued to wear it, with no intention of ever giving it away. Then I met Wally Ganyon, who later became my best friend. Wally was a country-music musician. I got to thinking how good it might look on him. It was too big for me. He was always admiring it. So one day, remembering what Peter had done, I took it off and passed it to Wally. "Try it on," I told him. It fitted him perfectly—in every sense of the word.

Like me when I received it, he was very appreciative and he wore it everywhere, including his photo shoots and gigs. Wally died in a motor vehicle collision in 1982. I was a pallbearer at his funeral, but I waited a few years before contacting his family about the jacket. I would have liked to have had the jacket to wear it again. I waited too long. They told me that they looked everywhere, but it had disappeared.

I wanted another one, even if it did not carry the same memories or the DNA of my friends. In 1989, I saw one that I liked and bought it. I wore it for years. Then, several years ago, I went down in weight from 210 to 175 pounds and it was too big for me.

I gave it to my friend Jethro (Jeff Sturgeon). A few months later, he gave it back to me. (He is bigger than me, bigger than I was before I lost all the weight, and it was too tight on him.) He didn't want to see it go to waste. If I offer to give you something, it's not because I don't want that item anymore or that I believe that you're needy. That's called charity. It's because I think you will enjoy it as much or even more than I have.

I have only one picture of the dark coat and Wally is wearing it. The other two photos are of me and Jethro wearing the newer one. It's too small for Jethro and now too big for me. So if you are my friend, and see me wearing a fringed buckskin jacket that you *really* like, maybe you should go on about how good it looks on me.

PICKING
the
MUSICAL WINNERS

A pivotal time in music came for me in the mid-1960s. In the early 1960s, I was focused almost entirely on Bob Dylan and the rest of the folk community of singers. Then along came The Beatles. I didn't care much for their earliest recordings. They were what many then called "bubble gum" music. They evolved quickly though, and I love their later songs.

I enjoyed rock'n'roll but I liked songs with strong lyrics, lyrics that expressed deeper thoughts, feelings, or personal angst than the cutesy "holding hands and kissing" words I heard in so many pop songs.

During the mid-1960s, I was driving along one day and heard, for the first time, Glen Campbell's "Gentle on My Mind." I pulled over to the side of the road and cranked up the radio. At the end of the song, as the DJ was introducing the next record, I made a prophetic statement: "This guy is going to be *BIG!*"

I was alone at the time, so no one can confirm that. It happened, though, and later that day I bought Glen's first record. Same thing occurred when I first heard Neil Diamond's "Solitary Man." Blown away again, and, yes, I was right again.

When I first heard the Byrds' version of Dylan's "Mr. Tambourine Man," I had that exact reaction. Wow! There may have been others, at the time, but those are three of four "first times" which I remember. And they *all* became big names in the music industry.

With the *fourth one*, though, I didn't even know how big she became until 50 years later! It was back in the centennial year, 1967, perhaps on Victoria Day, or the Dominion Day holiday, I'm not sure which. A long flat-bed trailer was set up down at the end of Brant Street, in Burlington, Ontario, where I was living at the time. A band which I didn't know had set up their equipment and were about to perform for the crowd. A buddy and I arrived just as they were ready to start.

An attractive, young Black girl working keyboards took the mic and began to sing. We were walking by but she stopped me dead in my tracks. She looked about 18 or so years old. I thought she was some famous singer whom I didn't recognize. Her voice and her stage presence were so professional, so stunning, that I was transfixed.

My friend didn't know the name of the band or the singer, but we asked someone nearby. He said her name was Brenda Gordon, the band was from Toronto, and if memory serves, they were called the Misfits or something like that. We listened for a while, but my friend wanted to get some beer, so we continued up the street to the Sherwood Inn. Once we had our fill of draft beer, we went back down Brant Street, but the band had already packed up and gone. I remember telling him what I'd said of others, "She is going to be *big*!"

I never heard of the band after that, but I certainly didn't forget the name Brenda Gordon—or her performance that morning. Ten years later, I wondered why she had never made it big. Then, *50 years later*, I was at my computer one night and decided to Google her name—to see if she had ever recorded an album.

Surprise, surprise! I found her! She was no longer Brenda Gordon—but had made it *real big* as a singer, songwriter, keyboardist, and actress. Shortly after I'd seen her, she had married and went by the name Brenda *Russell*. I knew the name, of course, but didn't know they were one and the same.

Brenda Russell recorded her own music but she also wrote songs for the likes of Stevie Wonder, Michael MacDonald, and Roberta Flack. She was a regular singer on the Flip Wilson TV show. She sang backup for Elton John, Neil Sedaka, and others. She was also a cast member of the musical *Hair* in the Toronto production.

A friend of mine, Brenda (by coincidence), recently mentioned something about Brenda Russell in a Facebook post. I contacted her (my Brenda) and she filled me in a bit more. When my friend was 10 years old, and in Grade 5, she and her family moved to a new subdivision in Burlington, where they knew no one.

In the unit next to them lived the Gordons! The two families became fast friends. She remembers Brenda Gordon, who was six years older than she was, down-to-earth, happy, and very kind. Brenda Gordon, in a sense, adopted her namesake as a little sister. She handed down "lots of cool clothes," which my Brenda altered to make them fit. By the time she got to high school, Brenda Gordon had graduated. She also remembers that Gordon was the first Black cheerleader at M.M. Robinson High School.

Congratulations Brenda Gordon (Russell). Wish I'd stuck around and met you after that show in 1967.

SELF SERVE—
HEP-UR-SEF

According to my research, the first self-serve gas station in North America opened in Los Angeles in 1947 and, by the mid-1950s, they had become common across the US. But where I was living at the time in Ontario, I didn't see one until the late 1960s.

The first one I encountered was on a trip to Mexico in the mid-1960s. We were driving a VW Karman Ghia, which had a 10-gallon tank and very good gas mileage. Somewhere in Texas we were sucking air, needing fuel badly. We came across a Hep-Ur-Sef gas station.

It was little more than a set of pumps, a wooden canopy over them, and a kiosk where an attendant sat and made change. You put in your coins like you would in any vending machine and when you'd pumped that value in gas, the pump stopped. The price of gas was then about 30 cents a gallon—but here at the Hep-Ur-Sef it was 25 cents. Two dollars or $2.40 filled our tank! I thought that this was the neatest thing I'd ever seen.

At its peak, this Hep-Ur-Sef Oil Co. had over 100 stations spread across eight states. They sold out in 1972 or 1973. Pay-at-the-pump—years ahead of its time—no computer necessary. And you didn't have to walk into a convenience store where the disinterested clerk looks at you and deadpans the greeting "Didjahavanygas?"

THE MAGIC
of
FIREWOOD

To some, the cutting, splitting, stacking, and burning of firewood is simply a necessity—a drudgery which they would do anything to avoid. For as long as I can remember, though, it has been magic. As a young boy, along with the "duties" above, it was my job to fill the woodbox nightly and light the kitchen wood stove every morning.

We each had our chores to do after school and my first one was filling the woodbox. I always filled it before having an after-school snack. I had almost forgotten this, but my mother reminded me when she was 87. She remembered, and I remember, the different smells of the wood burning—the sweet smell of apple, the spicy of cedar, the earthy of oak, and the crackle of birch.

To me, the making of firewood—against a long, hard winter in those big, cold, uninsulated houses—was my contribution to survival, like my mother's. The canning of hundreds of jars of jams, jellies, fruit, and vegetables in the summer heat on that wood stove, now sat on shelves above the dirt floor basement, waiting for winter.

Making firewood is therapeutic too. I was having a bad time with myself one year, stressed to the limit and ready to snap. I drove from Moncton to PEI and spent a few days splitting a nice pile of birch at my friend Dr. Dingwell's house. I started to feel better.

To most, the day of firewood has passed and, when they need heat, they have only to turn up the thermostat. But there's something special about the smell and the warmth of it. I'd have little trouble falling in love with anyone who feels the way I do about firewood.

THE OLD
GARVEY PRICER

_____

In retail businesses today, having red or black ink on your hands means that you have had a loss or a profit, respectively. Fifty years ago, *purple* ink on your hands meant that you probably worked in printing or at retail, most likely in the grocery business.

We called them pricers, stampers, or markers, and we used them daily to imprint the price on products. It was *impossible* to use them without getting ink on you. Every clerk had one and most of us wore them in a leather holster on our belts. You were proud when you were given one, having graduated from "bag boy" to clerk.

New guys were given an old one, until they showed that they could take care of it and not break it or lose it. When you were given a new one, which worked smoothly and quietly, you knew that you were now a permanent member of the team.

Shortly after receiving my first new pricer, I was down on my knees changing a product tag on the bottom shelf of that narrow aisle, when a female voice said quietly, "Son, your ... ah ... *thing* is sticking out." I had the normal reaction when I heard this and immediately looked down at my crotch.

It wasn't, so I looked up at the old girl, quizzically, my face still red, and she pointed to my hip, while laughing. My holstered pricer was sticking out perpendicular to my body and would catch in her shopping cart should she try to pass.

Hair spray was about the only thing that would remove the ink if you were changing the price on a product or trying to get it off your hands at night. That scented hairspray had to be removed, very thoroughly, before you went to the tavern for a cold one after work or risk derisive snickers and glances as you breezed past the autoworkers.

My favourite memory of the pricers, though, happened years later when our area supervisor resigned from his position to move to BC. We wanted to give him something memorable from the grocery business. What better than a pricer? So the staff and I chose a brand-new one, had it plated and mounted on a plaque, and presented it to him on his last visit to the supermarket. He appreciated it and clutched it proudly as he left the store. That was around 1970. I wonder if Hank Boxtart still has it.

THE
WALTONS

In life we are all headed in the same direction, at approximately the same speed. Some of us, however, are closer than others to the finish line because our starting times are staggered. Most of us will limp or crawl those last few yards. (That's right, this is going to be a light piece.) I was in my late 20s when the award-winning TV series *The Waltons* debuted in 1972. I was 10 or so years older than the lead character, John Boy, who found beauty in his surroundings and the family's everyday life. But it was this young character to which I was most drawn, because he was a writer.

Many writers are shy or introverted or grow up in a repressed atmosphere. They take to writing as a means of expressing themselves or of escape. I was like that. John Boy was different. He wrote for the sheer joy of it and for the satisfaction of recording seemingly mundane events which brought an already tightly knit family closer together. I grew up in the country, but not in a family like that.

I continued to watch *The Waltons* through most of the 1970s, as I moved from an urban life in Ontario to a more rural one back on the East Coast. Then, suddenly, the series was over, and I didn't see a rerun until around 1990.

I was a father by then, and this time I related more to the practical, common-sense approach of John Walton, the father. He wasn't the writer, seeking the truth. He was the leader, trying to keep everyone pulling in the same direction and staying positive in the toughest of situations.

My third session with *The Waltons*, which began about two years ago, finds me now relating to Grandpa Walton, who is the philosopher and sage of the family. He has seen it all before and tries to guide the younger ones toward the right decisions. While John, his son, is head of the family, Grandpa's advice is sought on most matters.

I have to wonder if my focus has changed as I have grown older. Am I changing as I age, to be like the characters in a fictional TV series, or am I simply relating to the character closest to my age? Staying calm is what Grandpa does best—most of the time. I seem to be able to do that better now that I have seen the cycles of life.

I grew up in a large family of six kids, similar to the Waltons' seven, and we lived mostly in the country. But my family was unlike the Waltons in every other way. I didn't even know any of my grandparents, let alone live with them. Our father governed with a set of rigid rules and a leather belt.

If a young child should have to worry about anything, it should be getting good grades, not whether he will die and go to hell because he is naughty. Our mother had little or no say in anything. Our father made the rules. All followed without question, or face the punishment. As a child, I was afraid of my father. The two families could hardly have been more unalike.

Possibly I have a yearning for that fictional childhood of *The Waltons*. Most likely, though, I enjoy the show because the series illustrated three stages in life: innocence of childhood and the lessons learned, responsibility of adulthood and the burden it imposes, and loss of responsibility in old age and the gaining of wisdom.

Whatever the reason, this time I will see the whole series, start to finish, as I got the box set of DVDs at Christmas. I am watching Grandpa closely, as I know that he dies before the end of the series. With any luck, I'll make it past that, in real life. If I get to see *The Waltons* for a fourth time, in 10 or 15 years, I wonder to whom I will most relate? Probably I will have gone back to my second childhood and be focused on the youngest kids.

Grandpa Walton: "John! John! Jim-Bob took my ball glove and won't let me play!"

John Walton: "Sorry, Grandpa, but your walker slows down their game too much."

THE HOUSE
in
HOPEWELL CAPE

I bought the house in 1979 from a widow. After her husband died, she'd moved to a seniors' home in Riverview. I paid 19 or 20 grand for it, if memory serves. (Oh, the good old days.) It was in fair condition, small—but I lived alone at the time. Soon after that I met my wife, and when she moved in, we built an extension and redid the whole house inside and out.

The house started its life many miles away in Waterside, Albert County, and had been moved to The Cape back in the 1940s or 1950s. It had an old wood furnace that would drive you outdoors with the heat and an oil-fired kitchen stove that worked just as well with diesel fuel, if the oil man was late.

We raised our daughter, our only child, Laurie Shannon, there. Laurie Shannon was her first name, not hyphenated but not shortened to Laurie either (Laurie after me and Shannon after a friend's daughter). The house was too small, though. Even after we put a piece on, it was still less than 1,000 square feet. So, 10 years after I purchased it, we moved to a new, much bigger house.

But while we were there, a middle-aged couple stopped by one day and asked us if they could have a look inside. They had lived in this house many years ago, in its original location, and raised their two daughters there. We said yes, of course, and they came in. We let them have a look around and relive their memories, while we stayed out of their way.

Then we all sat down at the kitchen table and had a cup of tea. We asked about their children—well into adulthood now, with their own families. Those girls had slept in the same room as our daughter did. We felt an immediate connection to them when we learned that their two girls' names were Laurie and Shannon.

The house at Hopewell Cape, NB.

Hopewell Cape after the addition and remodel.

THE FLYNN FAMILY'S
PARLOUR ORGAN

The organ was built in Bowmanville, Ontario, by the Dominion Organ and Piano Company, which went out of business in the 1930s. The case (cabinet) looks very much like one in their 1905 catalogue. Somehow it ended up in Sydney, Nova Scotia.

James A. Flynn, who was the merchant in the small outport of Petit Forte, Newfoundland and Labrador, decided that he wanted an organ in the family home, although neither he nor his wife, Nellie, played. With no hotel there, they regularly entertained and "put up" Mounties, priests, salesmen, and others who would stay over and sail out the next day. There was always someone at their house, or nearby, who could play and add to the night's entertainment.

As well as buying fish and shipping it to Europe, Flynn had the general store, selling grocery, hardware, fishing supplies, and coal. His coal supply came in by boat from Sydney. Sometime around 1957 he made a deal with a guy in Sydney for this used organ and arranged shipment with the owner. The organ arrived on a coal boat, lying on top of his winter's supply of coal.

In 1969, during resettlement, the population was thinning out in Petit Forte and Flynn decided to move to Placentia and establish a business there. He brought the organ with him, and it stayed

The Flynn Family's parlour organ.

in the family home. Flynn died in 1970, and later his widowed wife remarried. The new couple kept the parlour organ until, after doing some major remodelling and adding new furniture around 1994, the organ would no longer fit.

Nellie Flynn's daughter, my wife, Katie's, twin sister, Mary, stored it for a time in her garage, but dampness is the enemy of musical instruments, so it had to be moved. Next, a younger sister, Genny, took it and kept it in her basement in St. John's. Then their basement flooded.

We were living in Seal Cove, CBS, at the time, around 2002, and we had lots of room, so we took the organ in and kept it there. By now the bellows cloth had rotted and many keys wouldn't work. It needed a complete refurbishing. At the time, there was a place not far away, perhaps in Harbour Grace, which used to sell and repair organs and pianos that was now closed but still doing the odd repair job.

I tried for months to get them to do the work, but they never showed up to look at it, much less pick it up and take it in for repair. I offered to rent a truck and drive it up, but they wanted to see it first. I finally gave up.

In 2008, we moved to Hillsborough, New Brunswick, and the organ went with us ... and on to Yarmouth, Nova Scotia, when we moved there in 2010. In October that year, I asked my wife what she wanted for Christmas. She wanted only to have the organ restored.

I found a guy named Dwight Mallory who lived in Dartmouth. He tuned pianos and restored old pianos and organs. A few days later, he arrived, on his fall trip to Yarmouth, and assessed the organ. He recommended against refinishing as it would ruin the character of the piece, and we agreed to restoring the workings of the organ and leaving the case untouched.

He took the workings out of the case, loaded them in his vehicle, and on December 17 he arrived back with them and put it all back together. I paid $850 to have the work done. The organ worked perfectly, and still does. In 2012 we moved back to Newfoundland and Labrador, and it sits proudly in our living room.

Still visible on the cabinet are the initials the Flynn kids scratched and carved into it. It continues to wear a brass padlock around one of the spindles, where an unnamed child put it and then lost the key. It looks a little rugged, but plays beautifully.

But after being beaten around for about 115 years, I s'pose I'd look a little rugged too, judging by how I look at 75. Katie is thinking about having a *complete* restoration done on *me* soon. The refinishing is fine, but I don't mind telling you that I'm a tad worried about what parts she'll want to replace.

CHAPTER 2

RELIGION

Few people ask which church you belong to (attend) anymore. Personally, I find it a relief not being asked. Few people even attend church these days, and fewer still attend regularly. Your religious or spiritual beliefs are your own, between you and your God, whatever He/She/It is to you.

Having been brought up in a religious environment, it shocks and puzzles me that so many people do not know that, if you are Jewish, Christian, or Islamic, you worship the same God! The Abrahamic god— the God of Abraham, is the god of all three religions. Many get hung up on the fact that some religions/faiths call Him by a different name.

Every language has a different noun for this God, even within the Christian faith. *Dieu* in French, *Dios* in Spanish, *Deus* in Portuguese, *Dio* in Italian. In the Islamic faith, in many languages, God is Allah. The Jewish faith has a raft of names for God as well. If one child chooses to call her father *Daddy,* another prefers *Dad,* and the third *Papa,* and each views him a little differently, do you s'pose He's going to mind?

GRANDPA GOES
to
CHURCH

I went to church one morning a few years ago. First time in a dog's age. No, I wasn't suddenly convicted of my worldly ways. It was a promise, and I chose a church that believes smoking is sinful. I'd said for some time I would go back to church when they put in a smoking section. I smoke, off and on, mostly on. At the time, I smoked cigars. I decided to break my rule. Why not? It's *my* rule!

Anyway, the service was different from what I recalled from my youth. I remember the old preacher, the even older organist, both with unsmiling reverent faces, and all those familiar hymns. Here they had an organist, a pianist, and a drummer. There was a bass guitar on a stand but no player that day. I was doing the bass line in my head, but at times I would move to lead guitar where I felt they needed it, or to assist the drummer.

Trouble is, I knew none of the hymns. Not even one—and well over half the program was singing! All modern stuff. The lyrics were displayed on a giant wall screen but not the notes. This crowd doesn't use hymn books. I could really not follow, or be on time with, the chord changes. That didn't stop some of the faithful seated near me from "singing" His praises! It really clarified for me the meaning of "make a joyful noise unto the Lord."

When I'm recording, and don't know the tune well, or am in the wrong key, I want to take a break and smoke. I got thinking about the cigars in my car and wanted one, badly.

About 45 minutes into the service, the preacher started talking about Nicodemus. All I could see in my mind's eye was the word Nicoderm, "The Patch," and the craving worsened. I wanted only one cigar—but that specimen was the size of a telephone pole!

There were about 100 souls out that morning, a good assortment of ages, a smattering of visible minorities. Some came to listen. Some came to perform. One lady was taking notes. I'm sure all were committed, and bless their hearts and souls for it. They are true believers.

But as I drove away after the benediction, I lit up a cigar and said to myself, "I believe that the next time I'll attend, in the smoking section, by watching one of those TV preachers at home."

HEAVEN HAS
AN EXPRESS LANE
(On the loss of a child)

You have just suffered the greatest loss any parent can ever know. You've lost your child. If you are a person of faith, your faith may falter. You may be questioning the unfathomable wisdom of God, or even His very existence.

There are no words? Of course, there are no words. There never were and never will be. There is, however, faith.

Would it help if you believed that God has an express lane where a chosen few are directed, for quick entry into heaven?

That chosen few would include almost all doctors, nurses, and other dedicated health workers, first responders, police, firefighters, those who serve in our armed forces, social workers, priests, rabbis, preachers, and all others who have spent their life in the service of others.

No questions would be asked. They have done enough good in their lives that He sees no need to weigh it against the bad.

A second group even more special to Him would include innocent victims of war, those who have been beaten, abused, or murdered, and those who have suffered due to neglect or sickness or hunger or other wrongs and eventually succumbed; and a third group would be made up of children and young adults who were not given time to find their way: "the most precious in His sight." They not only go through the express lane but are escorted by God's most trusted saints and angels directly to the waiting arms of Jesus.

If that is so, then I have to believe that your child went through that lane, and so shall they be forever with the Lord.

I can provide no evidence that such a lane exists. I've not seen it written in any religious text nor heard any priest, preacher, or rabbi proclaim it. Sometimes, though, one simply *needs* to believe, to believe in something that makes sense and is in character for the loving God you trust. Perhaps you need to believe this as well.

May you and your family find some measure of comfort in this thought as you navigate these troublesome waters in order to reach shore. Then, as you stand on the sand at the base of the highest mountain you will ever have to climb, may it give you courage.

And, in time, may you find peace.

The
DEVIL

The devil is a strange sort. He's a "quare hand," as we would say in Newfoundland. He's been around almost forever. Apparently, at one time he was an angel and led a revolt against God. He was cast out and has been trying, quite successfully, I might add, to get even ever since.

I don't know for sure if the devil invented sin or whether that's just an old superstition promoted by heaven's public relations department. He's a bad one, though. He tries to tempt people to do wrong; he even tempted Jesus, who didn't succumb. He has a red complexion and the uncloven hoof, appears to be hairless, and is generally depicted carrying a two- or three-prong pitchfork. Why would you trust anyone like that?

I've never met him nor have any of my friends, but priests and fundamentalist preachers seem to know a lot about him. That in itself is curious. Why does he not come around and tempt only ordinary folks to do evil? Start at the grassroots. Why does he spend so much time working on priests and preachers? How many times have we heard them say that the devil led them astray?

Usually, in their confessions, they imply that he goes after the best, hoping the rest will follow. Therefore, they have more temptation than ordinary folks and, clearly, we should be more forgiving and quicker to help them get back up on their pedestals.

I have a lot of unanswered questions about the devil and hope someone who's met him can clear up any misconceptions I may have and answer some of the questions that follow.

Why in the name of hell do we have a devil to start with? Why do we have this guy with horns and a tail who never does anything that is not pure evil? God hates evil and sin, right? So, why in the name of all that is unholy do we have a devil? God is all powerful and He hates evil things, so why does He not kill, destroy, or annihilate this scourge to His perfect world?

What's that? He wanted to give us choice? We wouldn't even know there was a choice if He had simply killed the devil and made us perfect to start with. Why did we need choices? Even as the flawed human beings we are, if nothing other than which is godlike and holy existed, then our choices would be from among Good, Better, and Best. These would be fine choices, wouldn't you say, if none other existed?

Where and when was the devil born? Did he always exist or did God create him? Why would God make something so evil that it inflicted upon us Hitler, Attila the Hun, Stalin, Vlad the Impaler—and all those other fun guys that humanity has had to deal with? If God didn't make him, then he must have always existed. That would make him immortal, no? He can't be immortal though, because God says He will overcome him and destroy him in the end. Why wait? If He hates sin and evil so much, why not just kill the patent holder, manufacturer, distributor, and retailer—the devil—now?

We are told that in the end of time, God will throw the devil, along with all those people he's tempted and made evil, into a lake of fire (hell) and either kill them or torment them all forever.

How is that fair? If you stole a nickel out of your mother's purse when you were five, lost it, forgot about it, and didn't ask forgiveness, you will spend forever and ever amen in eternal torment with the devil and Hitler for roommates. Why not kill him now, before billions more suffer and are sentenced to eternity in hell because of him? If there is no God, no heaven or hell—and no devil, then it is, truly, a pity.

We need somewhere *Good* to send, when they die, the beaten, raped, murdered, starved, swindled, and diseased people who had nothing on earth except pain and misery.

We need somewhere *Bad* to send, when they die, crooked politicians, ungodly priests and ministers, and the guys that invented insurance, interest, mortgages, bank fees, and contracts that cannot be read or understood by the great unwashed. The devil, as they say, is in the fine print.

So must I conclude that there really is a devil? If there is, then eventually there may be a little distraction for some of us—watching the truly evil ones burn. We will be burning too, but hell is bound to hurt them more than us. They had no pain or deprivation to speak of here on earth, but *we did* and have received a substantial amount of conditioning to discomfort.

TWENTY DOLLARS AND TWENTY-FIVE CENTS ($20 & 25¢) (This happened in Central NL)

———————————

I was driving home for Christmas, on December twenty-two.
After a long, hard road trip, some rest was overdue.
I saw that Big Stop Irving sign and my fuel was running low
So I pulled right in, filled 'er up, and got a coffee there to go.

I was getting kind of hungry, but I figured it might make sense
To keep my cash in my pocket ... $20 and 25¢
But I saw a sign said "Moving Sale" as I was headed back to my car,
And a sad young lad looked up and said, "Wanna buy an old guitar?"

His mother smiled and nodded, at the wheel of her weary van.
She was leaning back in the driver's seat, the Good Book in her hand.
The dishes and clothes that hid the hood were covered in gravel dust
But they helped to draw my eyes away from the faded paint and rust.

So I stopped to look and I asked the lad, "Are you really moving away?"
"Yes, sir," he said. "Going west, the week, if we sells enough today.
"Ain't got much left but this little vase and my Poppy's old six-string,
"I want 25¢ for the vase, and $20 ... for this old thing."

To call it a guitar would be generous. It was split and warped
and wore,
But I knew by the way that he held it close, to him it meant
much more.
"Any singer you like?" "Johnny Cash," he said. He started to
strum and chord.
"My Poppy said his voice might sound a whole lot like our Lord."

Then he commenced to sing, and I sang it with him:
He turned the water into wine.
He turned the water into wine.
From that little Cana town the word went all around
That He turned the water into wine.

Then I heard a voice inside my head, and the words made perfect
sense.
It was a big deep voice and *He* said real low ... $20 & 25¢
So I handed the lad all my money and I picked up that little vase.
As he slowly passed me his Poppy's guitar, a tear ran down his face.

I just handed it back and walked away, and through tears his
mother said,
"Now don't you ever sell it, boy. The price of it's been paid."
I watched them put it in their van. I remember the rust, and the
dents,
And that big deep voice saying low and clear ... $20 & 25¢.

CHAPTER 3

NEWFOUNDLANDERS IN THE PROMISED LAND

I was born in Newfoundland, then not part of Canada, but Great Britain's oldest colony. From ages four to nine, I lived in New Brunswick in about five or six different houses in as many different communities.

From 10 to 13, it was Nova Scotia in four houses in three separate communities.

These are childhood stories of going to Canada and becoming a Canadian, the funny stories, and a few of the memories that still haunt.

FROM NEWFOUNDLAND
to
CANADA IN 1948

I have no first-hand knowledge of how bad it was in Newfoundland in the 1940s. I know only what I've read and heard from older people. It had to have been traumatic, however, to pack up and leave all your relatives and friends and go to another country with no job waiting, with only the *hope* of a better life. I don't remember.

It must have been a long arduous journey in 1948. Seven of us, two girls, three boys, and our parents crammed into a 1930s sedan with all of our clothes, a few dishes, a few spare tires, and enough sandwiches to last for four days. You had to believe that there was something better at the other end. Since I had no schooling, no job or other means of self-support, I decided to go with them, like ya would. (I was only four years old.)

After two days of dust and potholes and changing flat tires, we arrived at Port aux Basques. We left from Port aux Basques and crossed the Cabot Strait on a vessel aptly named the *Cabot Strait*. The SS *Cabot Strait* was a ferry built in 1947 in Scotland to replace *The Caribou*, which was sunk by a German submarine with great loss of life in 1942. After two more days over slightly better roads, and grabbing a few hours of sleep in the car, we arrived in Saint John, New Brunswick, tired and dirty.

Forty years later I asked why we had moved to Canada. My father said that there was "a great need" in Canada and that he felt the call to go there and "do the Lord's work." He was a preacher and had been in contact by mail with a man in Saint John, New Brunswick, who would help us get started. He also felt, he said, that it would provide a better future for the children.

M.H. (Melvin) McCavour and his family welcomed us with open arms. McCavour, a well-to-do, successful fish merchant with a great sense of humour, was the man with whom our father had been in touch. Most of what I remember of him is from a few years later when we had relocated to other places and he came to visit. He would tell us youngsters stories, recite poems, and "find" quarters in our ears—then let us keep them!

His business was at the front of a wharf, and I remember he told us once that he was thinking of building a few cabins on that wharf. He would rent them out to tourists who could then fish from their window or door without having to go outside. He was going to call them Overnight Overwater Cabins.

His stationery had a logo of a fisherman, in profile, with rod and line. The return address on his envelopes started with this logo and the phrase, "No Catch 'em in 7 Days, Return to:" and then his address.

His signature took the shape of a fish. He signed all his cheques like that. The fish's expression would change from a smile to a frown depending on whether he was happy or unhappy to be sending that particular cheque. He would entertain us children for hours, with jokes and magic tricks. A welcome relief, no doubt, for our parents.

I don't know how long we stayed with them. They put us up later in their summer home. Then we moved to Manowagonish

Road in Saint John. My sister says that this house was almost directly across from the old Protestant orphanage. Next, we moved to another part of the Saint John area—Fairville. Let me tell you a little more about our family first.

My father, Roddy Gordon Pike, was born on September 23, 1907, in Sydney, Nova Scotia (we think), of Newfoundland parents who were living, temporarily, in Cape Breton. His father, Robert, was either working in the coal mines or at a steel mill there.

My grandfather (Robert) was from Lanceo (L'anse au L'eau) on the Burin Peninsula in Newfoundland and Labrador. He relocated to Stanhope, Newfoundland and Labrador, sometime around 1900 and married a local woman, Kate Clarke.

Dad told me that, as a child, his younger sister, Nora, wanted to be older than him, so they exchanged birth certificates! Both certificates noted only "child" (nameless) "born to," so it was easily done. If memory serves, he had to wait an extra year to collect his old age pension because of it. He died Thursday, October 25, 1990, making him either 83 or 84 years old at that time.

He left school early in Stanhope and went to work. When I asked him how far he went in school, he replied that he got as far as "the bird sings in the tree" in his school reader. He worked as a "cookee" and later as a cook in the lumber camps in Central Newfoundland. A scaler in one of those camps taught him basic math and how to read and write properly.

Later he was drawn to the city of St. John's. He went to work as a salesman, travelling the outposts of Newfoundland by rail and coastal steamer. He sold a variety of products, including dry goods for a Water Street firm, Halley & Company, a wholesale/retail outfit which operated a chain of stores called Arcade, in St. John's and area.

As a travelling salesman, alcohol was an ever-present temptation, and he fell prey to it. Most times, he told me, he had a bottle or two in his sample cases.

When he was visiting a new client and in the privacy of their office, he'd open up a sample case, look surprised, and say: "Oh my, it looks like I forgot to put this away last night," as he pulled out a big bottle of whiskey or rum. "I'm awful sorry. I don't s'pose you partake of this, do you?" As often as not, he said, the client would have a drink or three as he was explaining his goods, and he'd walk out with a nice order.

Afflicted with what he referred to as "dropsy" or "falling sickness," sometimes he would bleed from both nostrils and then pass out. One night he was down on Duckworth or Water Street, having a few drinks, when he encountered a church group holding a meeting on the street corner. They were singing and playing instruments, so he stopped to hear the music.

Soon the preacher started a sermon, encouraging the crowd to give up their sinful ways. My father was about to slip away, he said, when his nose started bleeding full force. He took out the two handkerchiefs which he habitually carried and tried to staunch the flow. The preacher saw him and asked if he could pray for him.

Without waiting for a response, he began praying. By the time the prayer was over, my father said, his nose had stopped bleeding, and he did not pass out. He told me that he never had another nosebleed nor did he ever pass out again—in his whole life. He said he decided right then and there "to live my life for Christ."

That was the beginning of his involvement in the church. He started attending services. I suspect it was the Salvation Army. He was drawn soon after to the Pentecostal church.

He did correspondence courses in theology and studied his Bible. Later he commenced to preach. He started congregations in several outports and supported his family by selling, door to door, anything he could. I don't know for certain which church he was affiliated with then, but he got ordained and had his licence to marry and bury.

My mother Alreta (Reta) Blackwood was born in 1909 in Loo Cove, Bonavista Bay, now part of Port Nelson, where her father operated a freighter up and down the coast and participated in the Labrador fishery. When she was 10 years old, the family moved to Trinity, where he had found better facilities for drying cod. Then, around 1928, when she was about 19, her parents Captain Ned (Edward) Blackwood and Ida (née Best) relocated their family to St. John's.

They bought a house on Morris Avenue, in a newer middle-class neighbourhood. Ned continued his freight business after moving to St. John's but gave up the fishery. He had several vessels, including *Mount Murray*, the *Newell*, and the *Hazel P. Blackwood*—the latter of which he later sold to Chalker and Company Ltd. The family wasn't super rich but they certainly wanted for little. The *Hazel P.* was named for two of my mother's sisters, Hazel and Pearl. He moved freight around Newfoundland by sea and had another vessel for hauling coal from Sydney, Canada.

My mother's two brothers, Jack and Walter, later became sea captains. She also had four sisters: Sadie, who became Sadie Hawkins; Pearl, who became Pearl Davis; Hazel, who never married; and Reta's twin sister, Irene, who died when she was 14 months old. My sister, Irene, is named for her deceased aunt.

I don't know how Roddy and Reta met. My sister seems to remember that our mother said it was in the store where she was working. Roddy either worked for the same merchant or called on them as a salesman. It could very well have been Halley & Company.

I also don't know when they were married, although since their first child was born in 1940, it was likely in 1939. Reta had blond hair, blue eyes, and was a few inches taller than my father, who was about 5 feet 2 inches. She started going grey in her 20s, before I was born.

She did not have an easy life with my father. She hated cooking but did the laundry, house cleaning, knitting, and sewing endlessly without complaint. My father did some of the cooking when he was home. She baked bread every second day and did laundry on alternate ones. She graduated from a tub and washboard, using homemade lye soap, to an old wringer-washer in places where we had electricity. The water had to be drawn from an outside hand pump and heated on a wood stove.

Clothes were hung outdoors to dry for most of the year. In winter, she sometimes brought in clothes that were frozen stiff—long underwear, pants, and shirts that looked like the paper cut-outs a child would use to dress her cardboard doll. They were then hung up in the kitchen to thaw and dry. Her life was filled with too much drudgery and too little love or appreciation. It hardened her in later life. She played piano or organ in church, whichever was there. Sometimes she and my father sang duets. I never heard her sing anything except hymns until she was much older.

She never drove a car, never tasted liquor, never smoked a cigarette, and never dated another man in her entire life. She told me, in her later years, that her favourite actor was Nelson Eddy and her favourite song was "Somewhere over the Rainbow."

She had seen "talkies" (movies) before she married my father, but not after. There were precious few rainbows in her life that didn't mean "The rain has stopped, girl, go hang out another wash."

I came home to visit her once from Ontario, when I was in my 20s. She was then living in Halifax. They had a piano where she was staying, but she was there alone at the time. She sat at the piano and played and sang "Over the Rainbow" for me. For those few minutes, her face brightened and she looked and sounded decades younger. To this day, I cannot hear that song without tearing up.

My first memory of any of my siblings is of my older brother Bob sitting at the kitchen table and waving around a sharp butcher knife. He said he was going to split an atom and scared the hell out of me by saying what that would do. I could grasp what he was saying but was too young to understand that you couldn't do it with a knife.

It didn't work, obviously, but he tried it again and again, telling the other kids, "I can make it work now," and scaring us again. Bob was not a bad person, just having a little fun at our expense. I include this incident only to illustrate that when you are very young, you can become terrified of harmless things, simply because you do not understand.

Bob, the great physicist, was four years my elder. Tall, with brown hair and brown eyes, he was usually quiet and studious and rarely got into trouble. Next in age was Irene, three years older than me, with green eyes, her mother's fair hair, and an outgoing personality.

Hazel, one year and three months older than me, had brown hair, brown eyes, and was shyer. She had a little difficulty with schoolwork. In Grade 9, I caught up with her. In Grade 10, she dropped out of school to get married. I joked with her that someday

I would catch up with her in age too. I had no way of knowing that that terrible day would come. Next in age was me. The youngest (at that time) was Doug, about two years my junior.

I was named Laurie Blackwood after my mother's side of the family—Blackwood, I mean. I don't know where the Laurie came from. Perhaps they chose a neutral name that they could use whether I turned out male or female.

Years later when I needed an original birth certificate, I called St. John's. The one I had identified me as female. Buddy in St. John's said, "No odds, just use White-Out, and cover the *Fe*, sure. You'll be standing right in front of them and they'll be after seeing that you're a man. We gets this stuff all the time, where a clerk guesses your sex by your first name. Get them to call me, if ye has any trouble." I had no trouble.

LIVING IN FAIRVILLE
and on to
KILLAM'S MILLS

Fairville later became Lancaster and is now part of Saint John West. In Fairville, we lived in part of a big house on a street with huge trees and paved sidewalks. It was there I had my first package of Planter's Peanuts and my first box of Cracker Jacks. I've had a weakness for both ever since. I vaguely recall my older sisters playing hopscotch on the sidewalk. Except for those memories, my only other one from those days is of an older woman who came to visit us sometimes. She may have been the landlady.

I associate her with purple because she always wore something in that colour—a coat, a hat, or a scarf. I believe my father called her *Sister* Stillwell, so I presume she was a church lady. She had an illness that caused her head to move, involuntarily, side to side, then suddenly up and down, like someone constantly changing their mind. I don't recall who, but one of us started calling her "Indecision."

It seemed like we were hardly unpacked there when it came time to move again. I hated packing for moves but even then, at about age seven, we all had to help. In those days, renters supplied their own linoleum or oilcloth, as we called it. It was thin and not very flexible, especially when cold.

After a few *more* moves, I got good at popping the tacks with a kitchen knife or a screwdriver, doing minimal damage to the flooring. From then on, it was my job to take up these coverings, roll them tight, then tie with rope, strips of cloth, or worn-out nylons.

We must have looked like an earlier version of the Beverly Hillbillies in many of our moves. We never made it to Hollywood, though, and the new place was often less attractive than the previous one.

Although I had become a Canadian citizen at 11:59 p.m. on March 31, 1949, I was aware that we were considered different because of the way we talked. My mother had a slight Irish accent, but my father had that old west coast of England accent because he grew up in Central Newfoundland. He dropped his *H* where it was really needed and put it back on another word where it was not. I ended up speaking like my father.

On top of talking funny, we dressed funny too. In an ideal world, the new and the different would be brought into the group to enrich it. In the real world, kids can be cruel. When someone at school asked where we were from, I didn't want to say. They knew, though, that we were from away and not one of them. We got teased and picked on by some of the kids. Naturally, I got into some fights.

At first, I'd give in and the fight would be over, but the bullying and teasing continued. As I got older, I learned to fight back. After winning a fight with a boy your own size, or bigger, you became accepted and left alone. The trick was to anticipate the first blow, block it, then counterpunch, and swarm the guy, hitting him with everything you could muster. You had to stay calm even if you got hurt. Lose your temper, lose the fight. Soon, he backed away or ran off. If you were lucky, there were no marks on your face. If there were, you could expect another beating when you got home. Done, presumably, to teach you that beating someone was wrong. Soon the other boys at school left me alone and too soon we'd move again and I had to work my way up through the ranks once more.

From Fairville we went to Killam's Mills. I remember nothing of that community at all, except a vague picture of some kind of church where my father preached. We were there only a few months.

Moving was disruptive, and we did it without regard to the school year. The new school sometimes had different books or an emphasis on different subjects. It was a pain. Making new friends in the new place wasn't easy for me, nor was saying goodbye to old friends you believed you'd never see again, and didn't.

When I look back at it now, as an old man, I believe that all the moves broadened our experience, but on the down side we didn't have the lifelong friends we might have otherwise.

In times past, many grew up in one community, went away to college, came back, got a job, and settled down in their hometown. Others never left. They simply went to work. A few kids even stayed in the same house where they grew up and took over the homeplace when their parents grew old or died.

Growing up, I lived in 20 different houses in 10 communities in three provinces. I attended a total of 11 schools in two provinces by the time I graduated. Then I went to the US and later Ontario before I came back east and bought my first house when I was 33.

Since that time, I've moved and bought and sold houses nine times in three provinces. We could buy a real nice place with only the money we've spent on real estate commissions. When someone asks, "So, where are you from?" I have to think before I respond. Do they mean, Where do you live now? Where were you born? or Where did you grow up?

I often claim Yarmouth, Nova Scotia, as my hometown because that is where I went to high school, but I know only a handful of people there anymore. All the other places I've lived are the same; I know few or none that live there now.

Today I live in a small Newfoundland community called Placentia, where my wife grew up. She hadn't lived here since she was 20. She was living in St. John's when I met her and then moved to the mainland with me. It's her hometown, though, and the reason I choose to live here. It is remote. It does not have the stores, services, and amenities which I got used to by living near much bigger centres.

We figured that I would retire here and when her turn comes to get out of the workaday world, she would finally be here to stay. I'm retired (from my travelling job) now, but still, my heart yearns for other places—some place to which I have more attachment, even if I no longer know people there—places where there are barns, silos, farm animals in the fields, crops growing, a pasture with a brook or stream running through.

A "quare" Newfoundlander, I am not interested in mountains or boats or oceans, or large irregular shaped rocks. I am a "flatlander." It's where I grew up and where I long to be. Those are the places I'm from—small farming communities near larger centres.

In Newfoundland, I love the Codroy Valley. It's closer than anything to what I saw growing up. The Goulds is attractive too, if you could only block out the tall buildings on the horizon, the traffic, and the ever-encroaching city. I guess those days in farm country are gone for me. I'd better get used to it here, and let the others live on only in my memory.

The clear dark night skies, the frequent thunder and lightning storms, animals in the fields or barns communicating with one another, the fresh mown hay, the verandah with a rocking chair, tall stands of corn and grain swaying in the breeze, orchards fragrant in their blossoming, and most of all the peepers (frogs) after dark on the first real spring evening, they are all from another place, another time.

I either have to go back, which seems impossible, or buy a complete set of *Green Acres* TV series on DVD and pretend. When my wife, Katie, reads this she will probably get me a set for Christmas. She'll pack it and my extensive wardrobe of T-shirts and blue jeans in a small suitcase. Then she'll hand it to me along with my cowboy hat and say, "Here's your hat, b'y. What's your hurry?"

CROSSROADS
IN THE DARK

As a child, I hated the darkness. The world was alive during the day. People seemed to have purpose and control. The sights and sounds provided relief from thoughts and fears. At night, in the quiet all you could do was think and imagine. A sudden noise or movement was out of place and therefore a reason for concern. A pet walking across the bedroom floor, its nails clicking on the linoleum, and then pouncing onto the bed could be Christ returning like a thief in the night.

Around age eight or 10, I became conscious of having recurring dreams. The first one was about flying. I would start out walking and then, somehow, by willing myself to do so, I'd take big leaps and rise above all the other people around me. I'd be 50 feet or more off the ground, and everyone would be looking up and admiring my ability to fly through the air, land softly, and then go up again. It felt great.

The second dream, a darker one, was of trying to run away from something and being unable to make my legs work. Sometimes it was an animal from which I was trying to escape and other times a criminal, but my legs were frozen and unable to move. Then I'd wake up.

The third dream, which occurred more often than the others,

was the worst. It was a cold, dark, and quiet night and I was walking down a long, narrow, gravel road. I was lost and trying to find my way home. Then I heard the noise of some creature following me, well hidden in the darkness of the thick woods, which came right to the edge of the road.

Finally, I saw a signpost in the distance. Terrified, I hurried along but did not run, so as not to alert the enemy. When I got closer, I could see there was an intersection, as a faint light illuminated the road. I looked up at the sign and tried to read it but could not make out the names of the communities to which the arrows pointed. I would stand there, at the crossroads in the dark, and try as I may the words were illegible and I couldn't tell which way to go.

Meanwhile, the noise was getting closer, and then I could see a dark shadow approaching me in the dim light. I would wake up in a cold sweat, breathing rapidly.

When we had only kerosene lamps, the day ended abruptly with the snuff of a wick. One minute it was day, and there was activity and purpose; the next minute, stillness, silence, and darkness. Will He return tonight? Will He take me with Him? Is there nighttime in Heaven, or is the light always on?

In houses which had electricity, the day shut down in phases. The bedroom light was gone first but some light still came in from the hall and downstairs where the older kids were studying and my mother knitting, darning, or otherwise repairing the clothes we would wear tomorrow. She sang a hymn or hummed softly to herself. God only knows how she could. Our father was either away or gone to bed early.

Later, the downstairs light went out and our mother and the older children came upstairs and settled in their beds. Out past the open bedroom door the wall faded a little in the absence of that light. If you were lucky, worn out, and tired from school, chores, and homework, you'd go to sleep before your world shut down.

If you could not, then you lay awake waiting for the hall light to go out. Sometime later you'd hear soft footsteps as someone walked to the hall light and pulled the brass chain. Snap! Next came a soft tinkling sound as the chain swung against the bare light bulb.

Finally, silence and darkness. Then it was *really* night and I hoped that Jesus would not return in the dark. Then I prayed that, if He did, I would be chosen and He'd take me where there is light and peace. Some mornings I'd wake up and Bob, with whom I shared a bed, would be already up and gone. I'd panic if I heard no noise downstairs. Had Jesus come? Was I the only one left behind? I hated the darkness.

"Christ is coming soon" and "you'll burn forever and ever in the lake of fire if you don't accept Christ" were the two themes that, through all the changes of my childhood, never left my consciousness and were to affect the entire course of my life. I truly expected Him to return at *any* time, literally like a thief in the night, and on days when I disobeyed my father, I had trouble going to sleep at night and had those nightmares when I did.

I didn't want to burn forever "where the fire is not quenched and the worm dieth not" but I *did* want to have fun doing all the things that my friends were doing. I believed I was naughty because I was often told so and punished for it. Punishment taught me that I should fear my father, and, by extension, God.

My father believed in a very strict and conservative interpretation of the Bible. As children, we weren't allowed to dance, sing secular songs, play cards, read comic books, go to movies, or watch TV, when it came along.

We weren't to listen to much other than the weather and news on the radio. The girls couldn't wear makeup, slacks, or cut their hair.

Anything borderline that even *one* Christian might think sinful or worldly we couldn't do, as we had to set a good example and be beyond reproach. Swearing, smoking, or drinking would reserve for you one of the hottest places in hell.

I was about 12 years old, I suppose, when the thought first occurred to me: How do we know Jesus would be against activities that weren't even invented when He lived here, sins like smoking tobacco, playing cards, and watching TV?

If He turned the water into wine at a wedding, I guessed that He may have also taken a few sips to see how it turned out. If drinking was wrong, what was He doing making wine in the first place? If He attended a wedding party, there was dancing, no doubt. Who's to say He didn't have a few fancy moves Himself? If Jesus could walk on water, He likely knew how to get attention on a dance floor.

Our father certainly wasn't God, but he had the kids convinced that he was very close to Him and was His servant, so anything he said was almost literally the word of God. We didn't challenge it. We did what we were told to do, without question—or suffer the consequences.

We were *not* The Waltons. I don't remember being kissed except by visitors or old women at church. There were some good times, sure, but to me they didn't outweigh the bad by a long shot. I feared my father.

I think I loved my mother, but in my teens I lost some of my respect for her because of what she put up with from my father. As a child in the 1940s and 1950s, I didn't understand how difficult leaving would have been for her, in those times, with a house full of youngsters, no job, no car, no money, and very few of the rights which men had.

My mother hugged me sometimes and I'm sure she must have kissed me too, but I don't remember. My father certainly didn't. The fear later morphed into resentment and then to hate. When I went to summer Bible Camp at age 13, my father *did* shake my hand. That's as close as we ever got.

COLD HOUSE
and
WARM SCHOOL

Our father kept the boys busy planting and tending gardens, cutting and putting in firewood, looking after the flock of chickens and other animals which we had at times. The two girls helped our mother do the housework. They made the beds, swept, dusted, mopped the floors, and did the dishes. One day baking bread, doing laundry the next, in an endless dreary cycle like the caged hamster turning her wheel because there is nothing else she can do. There were mounds of dirty clothes to wash and many hungry mouths to feed.

We didn't waste much. Bottles were saved for canning and storage. Cardboard boxes were opened up and nailed to the walls of any unfinished rooms as another layer to keep out the cold. Any metal cans were cut apart and nailed over rat holes in the outbuildings or mouse holes in the pantry or kitchen. In the winter, we'd hang blankets in the stairwell to keep as much heat as possible downstairs. We would stog around the loose, worn, wooden windows with strips of cloth from rags to keep the drafts out. Old overcoats and blankets were hung over the outside doors at night, as well, for the same purpose.

Flour sacks were repurposed to aprons and pillowcases and passed-down worn-out clothes became cleaning rags. We burned anything burnable in the kitchen stove. What food we couldn't eat, the cat ate. What the cat didn't eat went to the chickens. Had there been a garbage removal service at the time, it wouldn't have been worth their stopping.

School time was great. I got away from the drudgery and the dreariness for a few hours each day and the schoolhouse was generally warm.

I would borrow a book from the library at lunch time, read it on the way home on the bus (when we took buses), read it again when the chores and homework were done at night, and read it all the way back to school next morning. I'd finish the book on lunch hour, turn it in and get another. On Fridays, I'd get two for the weekend. I read, on average, a book a day in my childhood during the school year.

It was a great escape. I could go to another world where all seemed to have much happier and exciting lives. It also provided a means to shut out others. Most people, especially readers, will leave you alone if you seem really interested in what you are reading. I did well in school, always first, second, or third in my class, although I was painfully shy.

We moved six times within New Brunswick in those first five years. I would always ask, "Can we take the cat?" Sometimes we did, sometimes we left the cat behind. I remember crying and feeling sadder about that than about the move. A cat was wonderful company, especially when you were sent to your room or sent to bed early. To my father, they were simply a necessary evil, good for keeping mice out of the pantry.

NOW
THERE ARE EIGHT

My youngest brother, Dave, was born in Sussex, New Brunswick, in 1950. He was named Melvin Allison after Melvin (M.H.) McCavour, whom I mentioned earlier, and Allison after Allison Galbraith, a family friend in Saint John. My father wanted a biblical name for him, so he started calling him Dave, or David, and it stuck.

I was only six years old at the time, so I don't remember much about that event. Now there were eight of us. A story has come down in my family that Dave was very sickly when he was born. He wouldn't feed. It was only a matter of time before he would die.

Apparently, my father had to go out over the road, travelling, so he made funeral arrangements before he left. The grave was dug, but the people of the little congregation got together for an all-night prayer meeting.

They prayed and begged and beseeched all night long and, come morning, little David started to feed. Dave was referred to, particularly by my mother and older siblings, as The Baby until he was six or eight years old, as in, "Where's the baby, who's looking after the baby?" So, he recovered and came into good health. "A miracle," my father used to say when he was preaching.

When I was older, I couldn't help but wonder why he had had the grave dug, if his faith was so strong. I wondered too, why you couldn't simply ask God once to make someone better and it would be done. Why did we need to beg? Why weren't all sick people "healed"? On what basis did God choose whom He would make better?

Did it have to be a "good" person praying, or a "good" child suffering—or both? Recovery or death was up to God's will, apparently. But if God has a plan and nothing will alter it, why pray? Where is the miracle in recovery? Is the miracle that your wishes coincide with his plans?

ATTEMPTED MURDER
at
PENOBSQUIS

Our next move was to Penobsquis, New Brunswick, where we lived above a general store. Originally, it had been the living quarters of the merchant. Before we moved in, it had been used for storage but was no longer needed for that purpose. It was hot in the summer and cold in the winter.

I recall sitting in a chair by the window and watching big trucks, often hauling bulldozers and backhoes (we called them steam shovels then). These trucks were some of the few that had company names painted on the side at the time. The company was the Dexter Construction Company. Across the street an old man sat on his verandah, day after day. He didn't miss much of what was going on. We called him "Herb Breen, the Mayor," although he was not.

I remember nothing of the bedrooms or the kitchen in that place, just the big open area where we played or sat. There was an outhouse of sorts in the upstairs back porch. It was a two-seater, inside the building, and the, ah … waste had a vertical drop of about 35 or 40 feet to the outside back of the building.

Obviously, there was no splashback. Someone told me, however, that if you were quick you could jump up, turn around, and witness the impact. I was never fast enough to do it, and when I got old enough to figure out the math and physics, we were long gone and I had developed other interests.

At school, I got in trouble for kicking gravel into the open well that supplied the building. I didn't do it but one of the big boys blamed me, so I got paddled in front of the class. I was scared to go home that afternoon. One of my siblings told our mother, and she said, "Wait until your father gets home!" I knew I was going to get a good beating for bringing disgrace to the family. The only way I could figure out to escape it was to kill him before he could do it. I devised a plan.

After we got home, I went back outside, down in behind the store where the alders grew by the riverbank, and, using my jackknife, fashioned a bow and arrow from alder.

I found some butcher twine in the shed that completed the weapon. I don't know why I hadn't just thought to use the knife to kill him, unless it was that I didn't want to get that close. I was about seven or eight at the time, so the bow and arrow were not sophisticated. I believed, however, that it would do the trick, and, as it got dark, I crouched inside the back porch door, waiting for the enemy.

It got darker and I got colder, but my father's car still hadn't come up around the back of the store. Suddenly, the house door burst open and my mother came out, worried because I hadn't come inside. They had searched for me—everywhere except the downstairs back porch. I'm sure my mother had no idea what I intended to do with the bow and arrow. She and my siblings were so relieved to find me that no one ever told my father about the gravel in the well and my punishment in class.

The older boys at this school were real little devils. Our teacher was a young good-looking woman, and like most women of that time, wore long loose-fitting dresses. These boys would volunteer or take turns feeding the wood furnace in the basement. She always stood over the hot air register in the winter, as the room could get cold.

The boys said that you could see up through the register. They claimed that she wore no bloomers! As far as I knew, at my age, women and men had the same "equipment" down there, so why they wanted to look, I didn't know.

I do remember big, cold, unpainted houses, in those early years, especially the winters, most times with just a kitchen wood stove for heat. We'd use flat irons or heated hardwood junks to warm up the beds. We'd heat them on the stove or in the oven, wrap them in old clothes or a towel, and place them under the covers at the foot of the bed. You had to be careful that you didn't unwrap them and burn your feet while they were still hot. They usually stayed warm until you got to sleep.

I can still feel those cold floors on my bare feet and see the yellow ice in the indoor "chamber utensil." You'd have to open a door to see what it was doing outdoors, as the windows were opaque with frost. It was dreary. On school days, I couldn't wait to get away from the cold—in both senses of the word—house. If by moving to Canada our father believed that he was taking us to "the promised land," it sure as hell didn't feel like it to me.

HARCOURT
and
ALMOST "SAVED"

From Penobsquis we moved to Harcourt. A *long* straight gravel road ran up through the rolling hills from Moncton to Newcastle. About halfway between is the small community of Harcourt. That road, parallel to the railroad track, had a level crossing to provide access to the few houses built on the other side of the tracks.

Sometimes we walked to school along the tracks, which were raised and windswept bare, and I remember snowdrifts on the road up to the wires of the power poles. While the poles were not as high back then, these were still huge drifts. We had a church there and we lived in the house next to it. I believe this was a Pentecostal church, or perhaps some other fundamentalist group.

The population was a mixture of French and English, with the French being mostly Roman Catholic, and the English, Protestant.

One of the standard practices in those fundamentalist churches was and still is the "Invitation," also known as the "Altar Call." At the end of the preaching, the minister invites those who are scared by the descriptions of hell or filled with guilt for their sins to come forward and accept the Lord. Sometimes none will come forward. Other times two or three will. If a crowd goes forward, it is termed a "Revival." The Altar Call is usually accompanied by "Just as I Am," a favourite hymn in many churches.

The preacher then prays for each person individually, sometimes assisted by other "saved" members of the congregation. The new converts are then deemed to be saved.

Some churches believed in eternal security, so that even if you fell away from the straight and narrow, you could not become unsaved. Others taught that, if you backslid, you were once again considered lost and had to be resaved.

One Sunday night, I was particularly guilt-ridden during the Altar Call. Perhaps I'd disobeyed my mother that day or got in a squabble with one of my brothers. When my father asked any who wanted to accept Jesus to raise their hands, I raised mine. Dad then acknowledged those who raised their hands, one by one, all except me!

I know he saw me. Through squinted eyes, I saw him look directly at me twice, but quickly turn away each time. When he invited the others forward, I did not go, as he had not acknowledged me. I don't know if I got saved that night or not. Although I prayed about it a few times, I got no answer. I didn't feel any different. I still wanted to pull the little girls' pigtails at school and do the other equally evil deeds that young boys do. I never asked him why I was not acknowledged. Perhaps he thought I was not sincere.

Maybe he was embarrassed for people to know he had a son who was not *already* saved. He may have thought I was too young, not yet at "the age of reason." I never again raised my hand at an Altar Call.

If you have not heard an Altar Call or Invitation done by a professional, you have missed an important tradition in many churches and an interesting bit of theatre.

The old-time radio preachers did it too. Each put his own spin on it, and some got dramatic in their delivery with the rising and falling cadence of their voices, crying and begging the sinners to repent.

All the while the saved were shouting "Amen" and "Praise the Lord" and "Hallelujah." Some would speak in tongues—languages that they did not know—or their bodies would convulse involuntarily. Sometimes they'd even fall to the floor writhing. I suppose that's where the term *Holy Rollers* came from.

Most preachers told a little story or illustration about someone who came to the Lord and how it changed their life in a positive way. Always an organ or other instrument played softly in the background and a soloist or the congregation sang the hymn in a subdued voice to his narrative.

Occasionally, my father would record a church service on an old reel-to-reel tape recorder for radio broadcast. I have no recording of him giving his Invitation, but I heard it often enough that, if memory serves, it would have gone very much like this:

And now, brothers and sisters, while Sister Sarah softly sings, and every head is bowed and every eye is closed ... is there anyone out there that feels that special call tonight?

Maybe you're a Christian and you've backslid, or maybe you have never known the joy of a personal relationship with God. But you know in your heart and soul that someday you must walk that valley alone, and you know that there are only two choices ... Right or Wrong.

The time draweth nigh and no man knoweth the day nor the hour, except God, and you can hear him calling you now. You feel that tug at your heart, and you know what you should do. Just raise your hand as a confirmation that you accept Him.

I see you, brother, and the Lord sees you, and every eye remains closed, and you, sister, and you, the Lord sees you, brother, and you too! And the Lord wants you to come forward now, and every head is bowed, every eye is closed. This could be your last chance to seek Him.

Meanwhile the soft singing continued at the tempo of a slow waltz: "Just as I am, without one plea, but that Thy blood was shed for me, and that thou bidst me come to Thee, O Lamb of God, I come ... I come."

If the sinners weren't yet moved enough to raise their hands, he'd continue with a story.

You know, I was in a small community in Newfoundland a few years ago doing evangelistic work. Sitting in a cabin with a young man named Jim, I tried to get him to accept Jesus. The room was littered with cigarette butts and empty beer bottles.

"You never know," I told him, "you might cross the road tonight and be run over by a bus."

"That would be a miracle," he said.

"How so?" I asked him.

"Nar bus been down this road in the 30 years I've been here!" He laughed.

We saw a huge cloud of dust coming and got up to look out the window in time to see a big silver buslike vehicle, with a picture of a racing dog on the side, come out of that cloud and roll silently by.

I felt a momentary chill and the hairs on the back of my neck stood up. When the dust settled, I turned to look at Jim, but he was over by the kitchen table, pale as a ghost, down on his knees, praying.

That night he was at our tent meeting and dedicated his life to Christ! A while later, I saw the bus again at a gas station down on the highway. I walked up to the driver and I asked why he'd been on that gravel road.

"I got lost," he told me, "and I was so low on fuel I coasted with the motor off the last 5 miles down to the main road."

It was a tour bus from Canada, and he wasn't familiar with the area. "You getting lost saved a man's life today," I told him, and he smiled when I explained how.

The Lord does, indeed, move in mysterious ways. He will do what he has to do to save your life. Always has. Always will.

Jesus, the Son of God, walked all the way to Calvary for you, dragging His cross, as the crowds jeered and the soldiers mocked Him, and then He gave His life for you! The only thing He's asking you tonight is to walk to the front of this church, for Him.

Will you do it?

And to those of you out there listening by way of radio tonight, if you are at home, just bow your head and close your eyes. If you are out in your car, and it is safe to do so, pull over and bow your head. If you cannot, then just touch the dash. The Lord sees you and He accepts you. Thank you, Lord! Thank you, Jesus! You are moving their hearts, God, and they are coming to Your Throne, Lord!

And every head is bowed and every eye is closed and

they are coming to you, Jesus. The saved are coming to the
altar now to pray with those who have just accepted You.

The repentant would then come forward, often assisted by the saved, down to the front of the church. He'd then give a benediction, allowing those who wished to leave to do so.

And to those of you who must go home now—may God
keep you safe in your journey. See you next week. May the
Lord rest, remain, and abide with you now, and forever
more. Amen.

If he wasn't recording, during his sermon, he would strut back and forth on the platform. He didn't need a microphone to be heard by anyone in the room. After he got warmed up, he would take off his suit jacket, toss it onto a chair, and loosen his tie.

Later, he'd roll up his sleeves and adjust his armbands, all the while marching back and forth and preaching. Soon he'd worked up a sweat and out would come a white handkerchief to mop his brow. He always wore a white shirt and a dark suit, the pants held up sometimes by both a belt and a pair of braces and other times just the braces. I'd wonder if other men's belts served a second purpose at home.

Another practice common in these churches was "Testifying." The preacher would ask if anyone wanted to get up and testify to the goodness of the Lord. It was an opportunity for any saved person to say how wonderful their life was, now that they had accepted the Lord.

Some said only a few words, while others practically preached a sermon. One little wisp of an old lady, more ghostlike than human, who looked like she might not make it to another Sunday, always ended her testimony with: "and we'll gather up our hands and feet and go our fathers' God to meet."

It was a line, I suppose, that she picked up from a poem, or heard a preacher say.

I couldn't help but wonder, with what would they gather up their hands and feet since they obviously had no hands with which to do it? A friend and I had a good snicker about this one day, and I would look at him whenever she was testifying. He'd fight to keep from laughing and those nearby frowned at him, while I'd glance over innocently with a straight face.

LILACS, MAYFLOWERS, DAWN,
and
MY FRIEND GARY

I don't remember the move from Harcourt. My next recollection is about Petitcodiac.

The walk to school in Petitcodiac was past some houses, in a built-up area. I will never forget late in the school year that sweet fragrance filling the air, as we went down the street lined with lilac bushes. Lilacs are still my favourite flower, although the colour of the purple ones reminds me of death, somehow. The kids picked mayflowers in the spring, tied them in little bunches with twine, and sold them door to door in the neighbourhood. Even today, the fragrance of lilacs or mayflowers immediately transports me back to childhood.

At school, there was a cute little dark-haired girl named Dale. I had a crush on her but was too shy to even speak to her. Early one morning before class started, I left a bunch of mayflowers that I'd picked on her desk. She never found out who left them but she kept smiling and holding them to her nose for half the day.

All the kids got a Coronation medal when Elizabeth Windsor succeeded her father to become queen. I still have mine—the nicest gift I had ever received, up to that point in my life. It was brand new and shiny and looked like it was valuable. I would never try to sell it or trade it for marbles.

The old house we lived in was small with low ceilings. It originally had one big room and pieces had been added on, hodgepodge, as the original family grew. No maintenance had been done in many years. Set back from the road by a long muddy driveway, it leaked when it rained and mildewed when it got warm.

At one side of the driveway, at the road, was a house where the Robbs lived. On the other side was another house with a small canteen/store at the side entrance.

A French-speaking family named DuBois lived nearby. We played with their kids, the Robb kids, and others in the fields behind the houses and watched the trains go by. Often tramps, or hobos, would jump off the train before it got to the station. Sometimes they knocked on our door looking for a handout, a meal, or a job of work for a few cents.

We always invited them in, and although we had very little, none was sent away hungry. I wondered why they would stop at our door and not at the fancy homes of the richer people up the street. My father told us that they would likely be turned away, or call the police.

He said that if I should ever find myself in a strange town, and needed help or money, to knock on the poorest, humblest home I could find—a house like ours. Poor people, he said, knew what having nothing and no one to turn to, was like, and they'd be more likely to share what little they had. I have to admit that he was right, and I suppose I respected him for helping others. I'd lose that respect, however, the next time I took a beating and wanted to jump on the next train out. I never got the nerve to do it.

An elderly neighbourhood lady came to visit us sometimes. I don't remember her name, but she always had six pink peppermints wrapped in a handkerchief for us kids. As she doled them out, I'd wonder whether she had wiped her nose on the way over. Although I loved candy, I'd save my peppermint for later, but give it to one of the other kids.

In the fall of 1953, we moved from Petitcodiac, New Brunswick, to Nova Scotia.

Why did we move so much? I didn't know, and when we reached the new place there was never any talk of the old one. Our father may have given us a reason at the time of these moves, and it must have made sense or I would remember. Perhaps I thought that everybody moved around, seemingly at random, as we did.

I questioned my father on this when he was old, and he replied, "I always went where the Lord led me to go." I felt like asking him, "Did the Lord realize how hard it was on your wife and six kids?" But I didn't.

In Petitcodiac, my best friend was Gary Robb, who lived right next door. We'd pick up discarded beer and pop bottles in the ditches and trade them in for candy at the canteen. My prized possession was an old tire. A worn-out tire off a pickup, which you could curl up inside of and have someone roll you down a hill. You could just roll it along, too, using a stick to move it and see how far you could make it go without it falling over.

My father said there was no room on the truck to take my tire along with all our belongings. I rolled it next door and gave it to Gary. I can still see him as our 1938 rustmobile followed that rickety truck down the long muddy driveway for the last time. He was crouched down, the tire at his side, and he was hugging it like it was his pet dog or something. He and I were both crying and waving like crazy. I never saw him again.

I loved the next place: Avonport, Nova Scotia. I dream of it sometimes. I have no idea why, but my memories up until then appear almost entirely in black and white, in my mind.

Everything *after* Petitcodiac appears in colour. I see Avonport in full colour, the different shades of the green trees mixed with the yellows in the meadows and the marsh by the Bay of Fundy. I see the blue sky, with white clouds drifting slowly across it, and that mysterious little island just off the shore.

There were woods and fields to explore and a big old house with many rooms. The last house on the gravel road on a small point of land, it was bordered by rose bushes, lilacs, and wild hazelnut trees.

My father was then selling Rawleigh or Watkins products door to door. I recall the syrups—lemon, grape, and orange. We had no refrigerator or icebox, but on a hot summer day, on a rare occasion, we'd mix syrup with cold well water to drink. The wonderful exotic smells of the different spices he sold have always stayed with me.

I remember him saying that he told a customer where he lived, and they said, "What are you doing living down at the Point? Why, there's nothing there but snakes, mosquitoes, and John Crowell." It was like heaven to me, especially when our father was away.

Another quote I remember from Avonport came from a neighbour; it may indeed have been Crowell. A man was over visiting one afternoon and telling us about a local legend of buried treasure on the nearby island. "If I had my way," he said, "I'd find it if I had to dig up every inch of Boot Island." I decided to go there myself and find that treasure when I got old enough, and I dreamed about it day and night. We were in Avonport less than a year. My father came home one day and announced that we were moving.

In one of his best-known songs, "Willy the Wandering Gypsy and Me," Billy Joe Shaver wrote, "Movin' is the closest thing to being free." Perhaps it is freedom to he who makes the decision to move, but those bound to him by invisible, unbreakable chains are prisoners still, and are reminded each time that they have no freedom to choose.

AUNT HAZEL, UNCLE BOB,
and
NED BLACKWOOD

This move was only about a half-hour distance to a village called Hortonville. It may as well have been 500 miles though, at that time, with no money for gas, bad roads, and worse cars. We never returned to a place where we'd lived previously. We rented an old farmhouse in Hortonville with some outbuildings, fields, and room for a big garden. It was known as MacDonald's farm, named for the owner.

Up on the hill behind us lived the Crowells. Their son, Arthur, was a little older than me but I played with him sometimes. He had a pet crow that could talk! He also had a BB gun! One day, we were trying to determine at what distance one would be safe if hit by a BB. So we experimented at different distances. By trial and error, we made some interesting discoveries. I can't remember the exact distance now, but we did determine that there is a point where a BB will only break through the seat of your pants, sting for a few minutes, but not seriously injure the fleshy part of your ass.

We went to school in nearby Grand Pré. The walk was no fun on cold, blustery winter days, especially if your feet got wet or your mittens had holes. I remember one morning, as we were all hurrying to get ready for school, our mother was trying to find a pair of mittens for one of us. The old man kept saying, "It's cold out, make sure you find a double-balled pair. Make sure they're double-balled."

I guess this was a heavier grade of wool or perhaps some sort of a two-layered mitten. He said it two or three times and finally she said in frustration, "Oh go on wid ya, *you're* double-balled!" No one seemed to get her accidental double entendre but me, and it was all that I could do to keep from laughing. Fortunately, I didn't, as I'm sure I wasn't supposed to know the other meaning.

Our father, as usual, was not home much. He was either out selling or ministering to the needs of people. We had chickens, a cherry tree, and a few apple trees, and we grew lots of vegetables. My mother canned vegetables, which would keep all winter, and made any fruit we could get our hands on, into jam and preserves. She had always done this, but I never really thought about all the work involved until I was older. From Hortonville on, I remember that we always had 200 bottles or more in the cellar against the winter.

All of this was cooked and canned on a wood stove in the kitchen in the hot summer and fall, along with all her regular duties. My father snared rabbits that winter and they, along with the occasional chicken, provided the meat that came to our table.

We had a neighbour nearby who reputedly made moonshine. Apparently, Joe used turnips for his mash. That fall, Joe came over to our place wondering if he could use our basement. He had a bumper crop of big turnips and didn't have enough space to store them all.

The deal was we could eat as many of them as we wanted. He would pick up some as he needed them, "for his cows." We kids walked past his house twice a day for school but we never saw a cow or heard as much as a moo.

Joe picked up a few turnips come spring, but the Pikes had already made a huge dent in the mountain of turnips on the dirt floor of our basement. He didn't return for the rest. I suspect that he knew we needed them worse than he did.

My father had little income that winter. By spring, there were no other vegetables or preserves left, and we lived for a few months on not much more than Joe's turnips and rabbits. My father would snare rabbits in any month with an "R" in it, so we had no rabbit from May to August.

The first fresh food in the spring was dandelion greens, and my mother canned them as well. I still enjoy rabbit and I like dandelion greens, but I cannot stomach turnip. Sometimes she'd mash the turnip with canned Carnation milk. That was even worse. We didn't have fresh milk but we drank powdered skim milk mixed with water.

To me that just ruined the water. We even drank *canned* milk mixed with water at times. This, many years later, can still make me gag when I think of it. I hate canned milk and can't eat turnip. They simply will not go down.

I'd scoop a handful of turnip off my plate and sneak it to the cat under the table when no one was looking. With us practically living on turnip, you can be sure we weren't buying fancy cat food. The cat would almost tear your hand off to get to it.

Our Aunt Hazel Blackwood, my mother's sister from Newfoundland, came to visit us in Hortonville, as she had before and after in other communities. No matter what time of year she arrived, it was like a mini-Christmas. She brought gifts for everyone on behalf of herself and our grandmother back in Newfoundland. Aunt Hazel was wonderful.

Nearly 6 feet tall and slim, she walked with the regal bearing of a queen. She never married. She had a wonderful sense of humour. (Perhaps those last two statements are related.) I had met her before, but this is my first *memory* of her. It was not to be my last. Every year, without fail, she and Nan would send Christmas gifts for all of us.

These are the brightest and warmest memories of my childhood. Our mother would get a letter from Aunt Hazel in the fall wondering what we wanted for Christmas. We'd each make a list, three or four items long, from which she could choose. As Christmas approached, we'd ask our mother when we got home from school, "Did the parcel come? Did the parcel come?"

Finally, it arrived and, almost always, rather than choose one item on our lists, she sent most or all of them! Without Aunt Hazel, Christmas and Christmas vacation would have been a bleak and boring time. Even a letter from Aunt Hazel became a special occasion.

Later, as an adult, I sent her a Christmas card that showed an old farmhouse in winter. Everything was white with snow, and grey in the shadows, except for a bright red cardinal perched on the limb of a leafless tree. My note said how important she was in our childhood, although we saw her only rarely.

I wrote that she was so like the cardinal that brought colour and life to an otherwise drab existence. Later, when I recorded a CD in partnership with the Children's Wish Foundation (Newfoundland/Labrador Chapter), I dedicated a song to her.

My liner notes said, in part, that when her time came to be judged, all she needed to do was to give them the names of six little kids as references. She's gone now, but if there is a heaven, she would have entered through the express lane. I wasn't contacted for a reference. I s'pose none was needed. RIP Aunt Hazel Blackwood.

We had a cat in Hortonville, as we always did elsewhere. All had the same name, Pudgy. Most of them were skinny. The old man used to say that if you want a good mouser, get the skinniest, ugliest cat you can find. Why he called them Pudgy, I don't know, but I can only speculate that it was his bent sense of humour.

Why so many cats? Some got run over, the odd one got caught in a rabbit snare, others I suspect simply decided to move on to seek a better life for their children, tired of turnip, no doubt. Some we left behind when we moved.

At school, I met a boy who would show up with bubble gum, chocolate bars, and other treats that he would share with us almost every day. I knew that he didn't buy them, because his family was as poor as ours. When I got to know him better, Paul told me how he acquired these treats.

He had found a way to get into the village store through a back basement window. He'd climb in at night after the store closed and fill his pockets. He got tired, he said, of prying up the window with his jack knife. It would stick sometimes, especially after a rain, so he nailed two sewing thread spools onto the window frame on the outside. After that, the window slid up nice and easy.

Paul was a lot of fun. He was always chasing the girls and joking in class. He used to call our teacher, Miss Harris, "Miss Hairy Ass." We weren't supposed to hang around with him because he was a bad boy and, as my father used to say, "He will hang before he's 21, and you can mark that down in your day book."

I met Paul again, totally by coincidence, some 20 years later in Ontario. He was well adjusted, had a good job, and still funny as hell. There was also a set of twin boys, Ronald and Donald, at school. I remember them only because one believed in Santa Claus and one didn't, each trying to convince the other kids that they were right. It illustrates, I believe, how two children brought up in the same environment, exposed to the same influences, can reach two different conclusions.

We fed mostly "Layorbust" to the chickens. The old man's version of Lay or Bust, which he named after a commercial poultry feed, was made by boiling up the vegetable peelings and waste from the dinner plates in one big pot. When it cooled, the chickens feasted.

We named all the chickens: Alice, Ruby, Doris, Kate, Dorothy, and other names which I've forgotten.

Cooking became my father's duty when he was home. One dish he called Skillygaloo was made in a frying pan with various vegetables and anything else he chose to dump in it. It was never the same twice. Any scraps and peels went in the pot for Lay or Bust.

Sometimes he made a plain white cake called Dodger and a sauce for it with vanilla, flour, sugar, and whatever else when we had the ingredients. Boiled apples were standard fare—not as a dessert, but as the main course. Drops, as apples that had fallen from the tree were called, were cheap, or free if you knew the right orchard owner. All you had to do was cut out the stem and any worms. We had many meals of boiled apples and baked apples after Hurricane Hazel.

Depending on where we lived, my father either cut or bought our firewood. The boys sawed and split it into stove-sized chunks. Some of those big old houses took a lot to heat. To get through a winter might require 15 or 20 cords. All of which had to be piled up outside to dry, then carried to the barn or shed for storage and finally an armful at a time into the porch and kitchen woodbox.

We "banked" the house in the fall with boughs of spruce and fir around the foundation to try to keep heat in and cold out.

When we pulled away the banking in the spring, mice scurried off in all directions, our cat in hot pursuit.

These mice had not found a way into the house that fall, having been intimidated by Pudgy, or perhaps they snuck in to get food but chose for safety's sake to camp outside. We'd use the blasty boughs afterward for kindling.

While we were in Hortonville, my father's brother, Bob, came from Newfoundland for a visit too. It was in the fall of 1954. Physically, Uncle Bob was simply a larger version of our father. He arrived a few days before Hurricane Hazel hit us and stayed until after. Our place was not damaged, but there was much destruction in the area. We went for a drive to look around. We stopped at a store and Uncle Bob bought us each an Evangeline Ginger Ale!

Big trees, power lines, old barns, and outhouses had blown over. Any fruit that had been left on the trees was destroyed. Uncle Bob kept saying, "Shockin' b'y, it's shockin! A fearful amount of damage, it's shockin' b'y, it's shockin'!" His thick Newfoundland accent and colourful figures of speech made me laugh.

It was nice to laugh. It was always good when someone came to visit, as my father was in a better mood. Often visitors brought gifts, perhaps a new tablecloth or an ornament, or a religious plaque for the wall. Vegetables, or used clothing for the kids, were more common.

My mother's father, Ned Blackwood, died during our time in Hortonville. I remember that we could not afford to send her home for her father's funeral, and my father was too proud to allow her family to pay. Perhaps he was afraid she would not return. My sister Irene remembers our mother having to go across the road to our neighbours, the Beattys, to take the phone call when it came, as we had no phone. She came back a broken woman.

Inconsolable, she cried for days, if not weeks. I did not know our grandfather and I was too young, I suppose, to understand how terrible a time it was for her. My father's death would not have elicited many tears from me, so I did not fully understand the special relationship that is supposed to exist between the child and the father. When I got older and looked back, I was appalled by how cold and unfeeling our father had been.

The old man killed Alice, my favourite hen, to have for supper during Uncle Bob's visit. Our chickens, to me, were as much pets as our cat. I was told to eat, so I did and tried not to let on that it bothered me. I was 10 years old, but I never felt the same about the place after that incident—and after seeing my mother cry so much. I couldn't wait until we moved somewhere new again.

Partway through that supper, Uncle Bob asked, "Do you have any liquor?" I was stunned and waited for my father to reply in anger. Instead, he scooped up a cupful of the broth from the bottom of the pot and handed it to his brother. I'd seen my father drink it before but didn't realize that they called it "liquor" or "pot liquor." Real alcohol wouldn't have touched the lips of either of them.

I thereby discovered that the word *liquor* itself wasn't bad— just the substance, so I started saying it to myself when no one was around, "likker, likker, likker." Later I applied that knowledge to other "bad" words, which I was hearing at school. I asked one of the other boys in the schoolyard, "Got any cigarettes on ya?" He didn't, but he started looking up to me for the brave young man I was becoming.

Finally, the time to move came again. I was excited. I hoped the new place would be better and my mother would not have to work so hard, and my father would be happier and better tempered.

I had a bag of marbles, most of which I had won during recess at school. I figured there would be so many interesting things to do at the new place that I wouldn't need them. I threw one at a time up on the roof of the house and watched as they rolled down into the wooden eavestrough. Someday, I guessed, a heavy rain would bring them down the drainpipe for another child. I remember this so clearly, because I soon regretted it when we moved to the next place.

Then came moving day. The following is how I remember events that morning.

Pudgy pranced back and forth on the verandah—jumped up on one windowsill, over to the next, and then back down to the front door—over and over. She didn't understand why nobody went to the door to let her in. She watched intently the events happening in the yard, but she really wanted to get inside from the light drizzle.

In the driveway, our old beat-up car was jammed with Mom, six children, and assorted household items. On the roof rack was an organ stool, a few chairs, and other small pieces of furniture. In the trunk were two spare tires and Mom's treasures—her sewing, her dishes, along with anything else that would fit.

Behind our car stood an old one-ton truck—flatbed with wood side-rails and tailgate. It was piled high with our beds, mattresses, tables, chairs, dressers, and various other pieces of travel-weary and worn-out furniture. Dad and the truck driver were at opposite sides of the truck throwing ropes back and forth to each other to secure the load. Finally, they got behind the wheels of their respective vehicles and we proceeded slowly down the gravel driveway for the last time.

My younger brothers were crying about Pudgy up on the verandah. Pudgy had finally sat down by the small pile of breakfast leftovers and the tin can of water that we had left for her. She looked up at us as we proceeded down the driveway. Then she got back to what might have been her last good meal. I told my brothers that she would be all right. The Crowells would feed her and she could always go over to the Beatty's place. By the time we reached the road, I was crying too.

I don't suppose anyone would be mean enough to do so on purpose, but if you want to break a young child's heart, leave their cat on the porch of an empty house when you drive away for the last time.

M.H. VISITS
and
A KICK IN THE GROIN

I was 10 and in Grade 5 when we moved to the small rural farming community of Billtown, past Centreville, behind Kentville, Nova Scotia. There we lived above a closed general store. There were no other stores in the village, only a school, a church, houses, and farms. My father opened the store, and it seemed that business was good, at least in the eyes of a child.

I don't remember all of what we carried, but I know we had grocery, basic hardware and feed, along with confectionary and pop. Sometimes I got to empty the garbage can and take the bottle caps out of the pop cooler after closing. I collected them. My favourite thing was helping to sweep up. I loved the smell of the Dustbane which we used to keep the dust down when sweeping that worn old hardwood floor.

The kids didn't hang around the store when it was open. Only my older brother Bob and sister Irene helped out. My mother used to say that the customers didn't want a lot of youngsters gawking and staring at them.

Frequently, a company, or platoon, of soldiers from the nearby Aldershot army base would march down the gravel road on manoeuvres. They usually stopped at our store for a break. They'd eat ice cream or drink pop sitting or lying down on the grassy

S.S. Cabot Strait   Melvin McCavour   Edward (Ned) Blackwood

bank by the store. They cursed God and their officers, smoked cigarettes, and spoke of other sinful things like drinking beer.

They had a whole different take on sin than what I had heard from my father. I learned a new vocabulary of bad words from them, too, as I moved through their ranks.

I picked up garbage and useful information that wasn't in any of the books I'd read, certainly not the Bible. I didn't understand what they meant by *screwing*, but I figured it must be something sinful that some grown men did.

A steep embankment out back swept down to a marsh with a good-sized brook running through the middle of it. We'd slide on the bank in winter and fish eels from the brook after sundown on hot summer evenings. We would skin the eels and fry them, and I was amazed how they would squirm in the pan, hours later, while cooking. Brother Bob explained it was just the nerves in the eel, and the eel felt no pain. He had learned that in school. Still, it is difficult to enjoy eating something when you think it might move.

That fall I suffered my first and only sports injury. It happened by accident while playing with some neighbourhood kids. Two of us went to kick the ball. He got there first but slipped in the wet grass as he was kicking. I slipped too, and as he went down the

The Hazel P Blackwood   Uncle Bob Pike   The Marie Spinler

follow-through on his kick caught me a couple inches to the left of my groin. It swelled up instantly and started to throb.

They got me home and took me upstairs to my bed. We didn't have access to a car, as the old man was away, so had they wanted to take me to a hospital, it couldn't be done. It would have been no different had he been there, I suppose. Our father believed in being healed, not in doctors. I don't remember any of us ever going to a doctor or hospital in my entire childhood. It may have happened, but I have no memory of it.

My mother applied cold compresses, I believe, and finally the swelling went down. I still could not walk. Within days, the flesh got infected, and when my father got home, he applied some hot poultices to the injury to "draw out the poison." I developed a fever and began to hallucinate. I was seeing fairies dancing on the moulding above the door.

I survived that, and while it may have been only a few weeks that I was unable to get out of bed alone, when I finally was able to get up and go to the window, I was shocked to see that the leaves had turned to red, orange, and yellow from the green they were when I got home that first day.

A belief in divine healing came with religion, as did a mistrust of science. Jesus healed people, and if God could heal, there was no need of doctors. That would be like showing no trust in the

| McCavour Signature | Mayfowers | Elizabeth II Coronation Medal |

Lord. God performed miracles, including creating humankind and all the plants and animals, and could cause a storm to rise, or command a river to part to let people walk across. The sick could be healed and the dead raised, if it was His will. It was not for us to question how He did these things, but to trust and obey.

My sister Hazel broke her collarbone in a car accident we had while travelling to visit some people near Bridgewater. I believe that we took her to see a doctor while we were still there but, as far as I recall, not after we got home the next day. Our car was beat up quite badly, but drivable, and no one else had anything but scratches or bruises. Hazel had her arm in a sling for quite a while.

Melvin (M.H.) McCavour from Saint John, New Brunswick, came to visit us at the store. McCavour had a wonderful sense of humour, not serious most of the time like my parents. He would do magic tricks for the kids and tell us tall tales. I don't know for sure but I suspect it was he who loaned my father the money to open the store.

This, I believe, was the last time I ever saw M.H. McCavour, a wonderful man who was so good with kids, and who, along with Uncle Bob and Aunt Hazel from Newfoundland, contributed so positively to my childhood.

Our next move was less than 1 mile away, down the side road by the store. I have no idea why we moved, but we no longer had the store. I'm guessing the business was losing money, went under, and we could no longer afford the rent there.

The new place, lined across the front with large sugar maples, had a big house, fields, woods, and a barn to explore. It was the biggest barn I had ever been. Much bigger than the house, it was weathered grey, missing a few boards, and hadn't been used in years. Sometimes I'd go in there alone and sit on an old wooden crate in the shadows.

Barn swallows had nested in the eaves in summer but were gone now. The odd mouse would sneak out of a pile of old bedding and scurry across the dirt floor. An owl often kept watch on everything from his perch on the hay carrier up in the rafters. Some of the mice made it to their destination.

It was my quiet place where I could be alone. We didn't live there long enough to keep any animals or plant gardens. This move made our walk to school close to 2 miles. I was in Grade 6.

I started writing poetry while we were there, most often in the barn. I was fascinated by the more sophisticated poems I had heard the kids in the older grades reciting at school. I wrote one about the Sputnik satellite that Russia had recently launched.

Somehow the old man came upon it and told me that it was okay, but could be made better. He changed some words. I agreed with him that it was better but, truthfully, I didn't like him changing my things. It was no longer mine. I kept writing but hid my poems so that he wouldn't find them.

Christmas Gifts

CHAPTER 4

PEOPLE
I WON'T FORGET

Estimates vary widely as to how many people the average person meets in their lifetime. (The definition of *meets* varies as well.) In my *business* life, I have likely met 100,000. I probably called on 2,000 different retail stores and other accounts from Ontario to Newfoundland and Labrador. If the average staff was about 15, then that accounts for 30,000 right there.

If I add hotel desk clerks, restaurant workers, co-workers, office staff, warehouse workers, mechanics, doctors, nurses, accountants, designers, architects, that old chambermaid (Mabel) who always left two chocolates on my pillow instead of the one—because she knew I liked chocolate—and the odd policeman when driving over the speed limit, I may be up to 1 million.

Some I got very close to, and others I met only once. In each of my books I try to honour some of those who made a lasting impression on me. Here are a few more of them. Everyone deserves at least one page in somebody's book.

HOCKEY GALE
AND
MY MUSIC "CAREER"

I was a late starter at the puberty game. On top of that, I was shy
and self-conscious. As a child, I had a high-pitched voice, which
took forever to change to a more masculine lower register. Girls
seemed to like those big hairy individuals with deep voices, so I
tried as hard as I could to lower mine.

Then one day, I went over to turn on the radio for the news,
but our clock was a few minutes fast and I heard the wonderful
voice of Roy Orbison. The old man would not allow us to listen to
rock'n'roll on the radio, but he wasn't home and my mother said,
"What odds? I think that's opera or something. No harm in that."

When Roy soared off into those high parts, I had to turn the
radio up. I never got over the effect that "Only the Lonely" had
on me. It was not only okay to sing high, but the girls loved it.
Unfortunately, by then my voice had changed. I couldn't hit those
high notes and I never was able to do falsetto.

I sang in the church choir and for some time we had a Gospel
quartet of which I was a part. We sang around Yarmouth at places
like the Knights of Columbus and of course in church services,
including weddings and funerals. It was never enjoyable. I liked to
sing but not in front of a crowd.

I fooled around with the guitar for a while, but then one day

I cut my finger badly when I was repairing a broken window. It healed, but something happened to the nerve, I guess, and I can put no pressure on it. It's on the left hand, the hand I used for chording.

The middle finger, you know, the one you'd use in heavy traffic when someone cuts you off instead of saying, "well, bless your heart." The guitar is still in its case and hasn't been played for many years. I kept it for when someone came to visit and wanted to play and have a singsong.

As much as I disliked my old man, I've forgotten the sound of his voice. I thought it might be a nice idea to record a song so that the same thing would not happen someday to my daughter. Then I met Hockey Gale.

The first time I called on his store, E.W. Gale Ltd., at Millville in the Codroy Valley, I noticed a large section of musical instruments. When I got to know him better, I told him what I'd like to do. He had a studio set up at the time in his garage. He encouraged me to record a song and is probably sorry now that he did. Hockey is a drummer and bass player but also plays rhythm guitar, and banjo, mandolin, and other instruments, when you beg him enough.

We ended up doing two CDs in partnership with the Children's Wish Foundation and raised a few thousand dollars. Hockey spent countless hours recording, mixing, adding other instruments, recording backup vocals, and getting other local musicians to play the lead parts on mandolin, fiddle, and guitar. I owe him a huge debt of gratitude for all the work he did without compensation.

I got to know Hockey well in those many hours we spent in Studio1 (the garage), Studio2 (the rental house next door), and Studio3 (his basement).

We often stayed up until daybreak recording and re-recording a song, as Hockey tried different instruments and different sound effects to augment my mediocre voice.

He was kind and patient, listened to my stupid ideas without laughing, and I came to think of him as a brother. Still do. His wife, Gerardine, was wonderful too, never complaining about my pipe smoking in the basement, my sleeping on a couch in their rec room, or my monopolizing so much of what could have been their free time together.

When she gets old and grey, my daughter, Laurie Shannon, will remember what I sounded like, because of Hockey's kindness and patience. Hopefully, she will not die laughing at my voice. Thanks, Hockey.

Edwin (hockey) Gale and Gerardine MacLellan Gale.

SANDRA PHINNEY

It was on a Saturday in the fall of 1958, a week after school had started, that the Pikes and all of their worldly goods arrived in Yarmouth, Nova Scotia, at 33 Willow Street, a huge old grey house converted to a duplex. We'd rented one side of it. All weekend we worked getting the place set up. The water wasn't working in the bathtub, we had no washing machine, and most of our clothes were dirty from the work of packing, moving, and unpacking.

Worn out and weary, we overslept on Monday morning and hurriedly walked to school, with me wearing a shirt I'd been working in the day before and a pair of my big brother's pants. I could smell myself. We went to the office first to find out where they wanted us to go. By the time I got to my assigned home room, the door was closed and class had started. I knocked and opened the door. Every eye in the room turned as one to look at this strange little guy in his tattered plaid shirt and his baggy pants.

The teacher had been expecting me. She greeted me and told me to find a seat. The desks and chairs were arranged in pairs in about three or four rows. I glanced around but did not immediately spot an empty desk and chair.

Then suddenly I saw the cutest girl in the class wave me over to the empty desk beside her. She was short and had coal black hair, dark eyes, and a sun-browned face. My heart was pounding, I could smell the perspiration in my shirt, and I was embarrassed. I thought she would recoil—knew she'd turn up her nose when I got close—but she did not. Sandra leaned in, introduced herself, and slid her textbook over to share it with me.

She smiled and I moved a little closer. I was so shy and self-conscious I barely glanced at her. When I had calmed down and got up the nerve, I looked over and into her eyes and that moment burned into my memory forever. I saw only kindness, felt only warmth.

This girl was way out of my league, still is. I don't remember what she was wearing, but I could tell she was not from a poor family. The closest Laurie ever got to Sandra was that day. During any roll calls, though, we were close again as our last names Phinney and Pike were called, in that order.

It may have been at our Grade 11 graduation or the practice for it, I don't remember which now. They had us backstage and we were to walk to centre stage, one at a time, and then our name would be announced. The person sending us out had an alphabetical list, and the one at centre stage had a duplicate. Phinney comes before Pike, right? But after being sent out, and upon my arrival at centre stage to pick up my diploma, they announced Sandra Phinney instead of Laurie Pike.

The place erupted in laughter. My "friends" whooped and hollered. Sandra just tilted her head to the side and flashed that sweet smile and it was all okay. I don't remember if Sandra went on to university that fall, or whether she returned to take Grade 12 first. I wasn't there come fall, as I quit school for one year before going back to take Grade 12.

I left Yarmouth shortly after my Grade 12 graduation and lost track of her. In the 1970s I moved back to Yarmouth and bought a place on the Canaan Road in Carleton. Sandra was living nearby on the East Canaan Road. I had a crazy idea that I wanted orange-coloured burlap on the kitchen walls. I went to Sandra for advice. That's not all I got.

I don't remember who picked up the burlap, but I believe she dyed it orange, and she came over and installed it—a long, messy job—with much measuring, cutting, and sticky glue involved. I did little more than watch. (A word of caution if any reader thinks that burlap on your walls is a good idea; it isn't. You can't wash the walls and you end up having to vacuum everything but the ceiling.) It looked great though!

Later I decided that I wanted to make a set of banners for Wally Gagnon, a musician friend of mine. I went to Sandra for advice. That's not all I got—once again. Sandra picked up the materials, cut out the letters, and stitched the whole project together for me. I have no idea how many frustrating hours it took her to do it all, but she did it voluntarily and I became a hero to my friend—because of all her work.

Years later when I recorded my first CD for the Children's Wish Foundation in Newfoundland, Sandra interviewed me, wrote an article, and ran it in a local Yarmouth paper to help me get publicity.

Sandra got married, raised a family, became a teacher, a farmer, an entrepreneur, a social worker, and is now a successful travel writer and the author of several books. Eventually I sold the place on Canaan Road and moved to the Halifax area to be more central in my sales territory. Then, about 20 years later, my wife and I moved back to Yarmouth County.

Our daughter was attending the Yarmouth campus of Dalhousie University taking her BScN and living at home with us.

Sandra Phinney, age 15.

Without warning, the company I was then with, Ace Canada, got sold to another distributor and I was out of a job.

We sold the house and moved back to Newfoundland. Duke (our daughter, Laurie Shannon) got a room on campus and later an apartment. We were worried, naturally, even though she was an adult, as she is our "onliest baby girl."

I was going to call Sandra, but I knew I didn't have to. I told Duke, "if you ever have any trouble—of any kind, and you can't reach us or don't want to contact relatives in the area, please call Sandra Phinney. She will help you." Duke may not even remember this now. I don't believe she ever had cause to call Sandra.

So, thanks Sandra, for everything you ever did for me—some of which I've mentioned above. Thanks, even, for what you were never called on to do. I know you would've done whatever was needed because that's the kind of person you are, and have been at least since we met at age 14. Some people spend their whole life taking and end up with nothing. Others, like Sandra, spend their whole life giving, and end up with even more to give.

THE CASUAL WORKER

Many years ago I applied for a job at a department store which advertised for a casual worker. I already had a full-time job, in outside sales, but being a workaholic, I was bored when I was not working. I could do this on weekends, when I was off, and when the need for part-time staff was greatest.

The job involved filling shelves and waiting on customers. I applied by mail, and when I was called, showed up for my interview in suit and tie, the way I normally dressed for my full-time job.

At the store's office, the receptionist told me to sit in the waiting area. I was a few minutes early, so I chatted with her for a while and found that only two people were to be interviewed. Great! All other things being equal, I had a 50/50 chance.

The interviewer wasn't there yet, but at about 10 minutes after the hour a young lady hurried into the waiting area, out of breath and red in the face. She was a shapely young miss, wearing cut-offs and a small halter top.

Looking at me in my suit and tie, she explained that she had run here from her other job, as a lifeguard at the town pool, and didn't have time to change. She wondered if it might affect her chance of getting the job. I told her that she only needed to explain and it would no doubt be understood. I hoped I was wrong, of course. I wanted the job.

A few minutes later a young man appeared from an office and kind of froze for a minute before calling my name. He kept staring at the young lady while talking to me and I could tell he liked what he saw. I don't blame him. Had time allowed I would have the chatted the lady up and asked her to go for a coffee or something.

My interview went by quickly and before I knew it, it was over. The man told me they would phone me if I was chosen for the position. On the way out, I spoke to the young lady and wished her luck in the interview.

Despite my years of retail in the grocery business and a few years of outside sales in hardware, I didn't get the job—she did. But I did get to see the young lady again. I saw her some months later in a restaurant. We talked, and we went out a few times. She was now full time, working in the personnel department, having decided to make it a career.

I used to rib her that the only reason she got the job was because of the way she was dressed. I asked her: "Do you think I might have gotten the job had I dressed more 'casually' for the position of 'casual' work?"

"Yeah," she told me, "and when I'm the head of personnel, you come on in to see me, dressed only in your underwear, and I'll make sure I find the right position for you."

THE FLIGHT

I've driven her to and from that airport and others *at least* twice a year for the last 20 years—all told probably upward of 100 trips. Half of those trips are wonderful—the picking-her-up ones I mean—the leaving-her-there ones, not so much. The world is too big. If there is only a single digit number of people in the world that you care that much about, why do you ever have to say goodbye to them?

I try not to think about her (worry) when she's away. Then I start to feel guilty because I am not worrying. I know she's smart and strong and independent but that doesn't matter—she's still my baby girl.

Yesterday was no fun. We were up at 5, got to the airport at 8 for her international flight at 10:30, and when we arrived, we discovered that the flight was delayed an hour. Because of this there was no lineup to check her baggage—and no clerks either! She was the *only* one in line and we waited 20 minutes before a female clerk waved her over.

Her bag was too heavy, and instead of paying an exorbitant fee, she decided to repack part of it into a spare bag we had, and pay for two bags at the regular cost. She repacked and went back to the lineup. There were two clerks now, but she still stood there another 20 minutes or so. Finally, an older man dressed in an Air Canada uniform (a supervisor, I expect) came over to the counter, saw her, and opened a wicket.

Nice man. Friendly, and with a big smile, he told her that he would not charge her for the extra bag. She was tired, as she had been up half the night, so she decided that she would go through security now and try to get some sleep before boarding.

At the pre-security—where two ladies with latex gloves checked her boarding pass and ID—she got through quickly, took two steps, then stopped, turned, and said, "I love you, Dad," then turned back and disappeared into the enclosed area. The two ladies smiled at me and one wiped her eye.

I made it to the car, but stayed a few minutes before I could drive home. The house is empty now—without her stuff spread out, and the light on in her room. Love isn't supposed to hurt this much—is it?

Grandpa Pike and his "onliest babby girl," Laurie Shannon.

TRICIA

She was tall and slim and beautiful. Her black hair shone and her dark brown eyes smiled long after the rest of her face relaxed. I didn't know any of that at the time, though, because I fell in love with her on the phone. She was my boss's new executive assistant, working in the company's head office in Toronto. I'd call him from my sales territory in the Maritimes. She would answer his phone calls.

If he was busy or out of the office, she knew how to get the information I needed and either provide it while I was on the phone or get back to me. Most times, after she started there, I had no need of talking with my boss. She had it covered.

I fell in love with her voice, with her kindness and her efficiency. It was a business relationship, so I didn't ask her age or whether she was single. I found out, however, through a fellow road warrior who had recently been at head office, that she was young, attractive, and separated.

It was Dr. Dave Dingwell, our regional manager out east, who told me those things, and knowing the great prankster that he was, I was really not expecting to meet a woman so spectacular when I went to our next hardware show and sales meeting in Toronto. I was guessing that she'd be an older woman with grey hair, yellow teeth, and a houseful of cats.

Was I ever wrong! I invited her for a coffee after work on my first day there and she said yes. She needed to go home first, so I met her at her apartment later.

We went for a walk, both of us talking a mile a minute, asking about the other's life, hopes, and dreams—in our 30s, but like two young teenagers on their first date.

Suddenly, as we were strolling along, a seagull flew over and emptied its bowels on my head. This particular gull had apparently been on a very liquid diet as much of the excrement ran down into my face and eyes. All I could think of saying was a line I'd heard from a comedian who had been similarly assaulted: "For other people? They *sing!*"

Tricia laughed as she wiped me off with a handkerchief. I spent all my free time with her until the hardware show was over, and we called each other frequently after I returned to Nova Scotia. I was smitten.

Soon I invited her to move down East to live with me. Finally, I convinced her. A few nights before she flew in, Tricia told me that she had gone to a fortune teller. The medium told her that her life was about to change and that she'd be living "at the bend of a country road, in a small house—a shed and barn nearby—and open fields that rolled down to a big lake. I see a little blue car parked by the side of the gravel road."

I picked her up at the airport and we drove to my place. Her beautiful eyes widened when I slowed down at a bend in the road where there was a little house, barn and shed, and fields rolling down to a big lake. Tears welled in her eyes when I pulled in by the side of that gravel road, right behind the little blue car that I'd bought for her, and handed to her the keys for the car and house.

Tricia found an office job almost immediately, but it was lonely for her with me gone four nights a week. She had my dog, Muttley, and a shotgun which I'd taught her to use. Right across the road was my neighbour, Gordon Hurlburt, who watched over the place and Tricia, even more so, when he knew I wasn't home.

It had to be tough for her. It was only later, in retrospect that I came to understand how difficult she must have found it—a city girl—away from her family, friends, and familiar surroundings. I grew up out in the sticks, so I should have known how hard it was on her, miles from even a country store. Lonely, but willing to do this for love, she didn't complain—or maybe I just didn't hear.

I loved her, but I didn't tell her. The words to express that sentiment have never come easy for me. Blame it on my upbringing or on my stupidity, it doesn't matter. It only matters when someone really needs to know, doesn't it?

We were in town one Saturday morning, doing some shopping and the traffic was heavy. As we were making a left turn with cars coming at us from several directions, Tricia blurted out, "Do you love me, Laurie?" Instead of saying, "Of course I do," I said, "For God's sake, Tricia, I almost hit that car!"

She went quiet but other than that it seemed that all was well. We talked about other things and soon it was Sunday, then Monday morning, and I rose early, put my suitcase in the car and left to go out on the road before she was awake.

I got home that Friday afternoon and her car was parked outside. I was surprised that she was home so early from work. The door was locked. Her keys were on the kitchen table. The house was tidy but Tricia, her suitcases, and all her personal effects were gone. I knew why—I'm not that stupid. I called her mother in Toronto.

"She does not want to talk to you," she said. I tried again and again. She would not come to the phone. A few weeks later, her mother told me that she had moved out to her own place and had asked her not to give me any contact information. I tried through friends in Toronto but no one could contact her.

Several months later I sold her car and put the property up for sale. I didn't want to live there any longer. When the house sold, Gordon took my dog and I moved to an apartment in Halifax. A year or more later a friend said that they saw her at the old Eaton Centre in Toronto but didn't get a chance to speak with her. I have not seen or heard from her since.

Forty-some years later: "I hope you found a better man than me, and I hope you found everything else in life that you wanted and deserved. And yes, Tricia, I loved you. I wish I'd been smart enough back then to understand how badly you needed to hear that."

PADDY DALY
HAS THE HARDEST JOB
IN NEWFOUNDLAND

What about the premier or the lieutenant-governor, you say? You think that they have easy jobs? I didn't say that. These people have a significant number of staff to do research, recommend, and carry out their decisions. Paddy does not.

Tune in sometime if you are not a regular listener. I can't listen every day because I would get no work done. If I'm trying to write a funny piece, it's difficult to focus when someone calls in to say that their power has been cut off and the youngsters are cold, or their cheque has not arrived and they have no food in the house.

Whether it's an old lady who's lost the scarf her mother gave her, or a man who lives alone whose dog has run off, Paddy listens patiently and enlists the public to help. Most often they do. This is a live show with little time to consult, consider, and decide the best action.

Then there are those with mental or emotional issues, desperate, on the edge. Those who need comfort and need to know that someone cares and will try to help. They have been up all night and the words tumble out of them in a disorganized manner. Paddy has to be patient, identify the problem as quickly as possible, with one eye on the clock.

Next come the politicians and Paddy asks them the tough questions, the ones his audience has been asking him. The program, three solid hours, is interrupted for the news and commercial breaks, and the program is relayed to numerous other frequencies across the listening area, each station with its own local commercials to run. But the caller is only in the middle of what was expected to be a quick call.

Then there are those who call in simply for the pleasure of having their friends say, "I heard you on the radio." Paddy has to urge them along and be ready to cut them off when they use words that might be acceptable in the shed but not on the public airwaves.

Paddy needs to be part psychologist, psychiatrist, doctor, lawyer, social worker, and friend. He does the job well, the best I've heard on 590 VOCM or anywhere else. I listened to talk shows for 50 years, while driving out over the road in six different provinces.

I've heard some of the best. I haven't heard anyone better than Paddy. I was listening this morning and a man with health issues, no family who visit, and a cupboard full of empty called. Paddy knew where he lived. He'd been there before, personally, delivering groceries.

JIM BARKHOUSE

I have a memory trick in which I associate the name of a person I've just met with a mental picture so that I will remember their name when we next meet. With Jim it was a tepee—a bark house. Barkhouse is a fairly common name on Nova Scotia's south shore. (Another common name there is Rhodenizer. When I hear it, I picture a large construction machine for building roads, e.g., "Yeah Bill, we're gonna need a bunch of dozers and at least three Rhodenhizers to get that part paved by Friday.") But I digress. Jim may have a common name but he is an uncommon man. That is my point.

He has spent a huge portion of his life in the service of others—first in the RCAF, and later back in his hometown of Chester. He began work as a clerk at Redden's Hardware in 1971 and ended up purchasing the business in January 1972. Redden's, at 43 Queen Street, was an old-style hardware store, selling everything from a needle to an anchor.

I spent about 50 years calling on hardware and building supply dealers and can truthfully say that I saw few that could work like Jim—days, evenings, and weekends, stopping only a few minutes for a bagged lunch brought from home. And you won't believe all the things he accomplished in his spare time.

Redden's Dominion Hardware.

Jim was not opposed to a little fun either. I remember one evening in his office, just after the store closed. The Atlantic Lotto draw had been the night before. At that time, around 1976, the tickets came in little booklets of five, inside a sealed pouch. The dealer could sell a single ticket to a customer but any open booklets had to be paid for by the dealer.

Jim had several open ones. We agreed to go 50/50 win or lose. We checked each one against the winning number. No winners.

And then, caught up in the excitement, we tore open all the sealed ones too! No winners—not even one. Later, we went on to the other business at hand. I can't remember if I paid Jim my 50 per cent of our losses. If I didn't, he would have been too gracious to remind me.

In 1982, Lief Christensen took ownership of the business, and Jim stayed on as manager with him until 1987. In 2021, Jim serves the people of his area as Board Member of Bonny Lea Farm, Chair of Church Memorial Park, and Chair of Chester Basin/New Ross Lions Club. In the past, he has served as Ross Farm Museum board member, assisted in planning and developing Our Health Centre (OHC) and served as Chair of the OHC Foundation, member of Chester Golf Course board and Royal Canadian Legion Br # 44, Chair of Minor Hockey, member of Chester Fire Department, member of Chester Chamber of Commerce, Executive member Chester Municipal Historic Society, and (still) as member of Chester-St. Margaret's Liberal Association Executive.

As if that (and a bunch of other stuff) were not enough, Jim ran for Member of the Legislative Assembly (MLA) in 1984 and was elected as the member for Lunenburg East! He was re-elected in 1988 and 1993 in Chester-St. Margaret's, he served a total of 14½ years as an MLA until 1998, his last four and a half years as Minister of Fisheries and Aquaculture.

In retirement, Jim provided harbour tours in his *Osprey* for 19 years, gave narrated tours of local history, and of nearby Oak Island, by water. Jim still loves power boating, walking, and hiking and is an excellent amateur photographer.

When I first met Jim in the fall of 1975, I knew instantly that I wanted him to be a member of our hardware chain, Dominion Hardware. I entered the busy store and asked the lady at the cash if the owner was in. She said that he was several aisles over, down at the back. Susan, the lady with whom I spoke, later nick-named me Stone Face—in those days I didn't smile a whole lot. Thanks, Susan.

When I got there, I saw Jim down on his knees, sweating and covered in grease, fixing an old beat-up bike for a young boy. I stood back and watched while he adjusted everything, as the child grinned and thanked him, then proudly walked his bike out the front door. No money changed hands, and Jim likely missed the sale of a big-ticket item, while helping someone in need.

Later, I convinced Jim to join Dominion, and I visited him regularly and spent time with him at hardware industry shows. We have never been out to dinner or lunch; Jim was always busy. I haven't seen Jim in many years, now, but thanks to Facebook we have been reunited.

Whether it's a nurse, a first responder, a retail worker, or the only woman on the seventh floor with the key to the executive washroom (because she is the janitor), I have always been impressed by those who spend their lives serving others. Jim is right at the top of my short list.

Jim Barkhouse and Grandpa Pike.

CHAPTER 5

QUIRKS, QUIPS, AND QUARE HANDS

We have a substantial number of all three here in Newfoundland and Labrador. In these pieces I quote and sometimes interpret sayings I've heard, respond to a letter from an Alien requesting information on our way of life, and readily offer advice to everyone—even when it is not requested.

From finding a non-existent ornament, to learning from a young child, and the *ungodly* things my father used to say, I know—I can get on like a know-it-all.

THINGS
MY OLD MAN
USED TO SAY

Aside from that *H* thing—leaving the H off where it should have been and putting it on where it shouldn't—he also had a number of sayings which I remember.

If someone was sick: "He looked like someone who was sent for but couldn't come."

Things going wrong: "What you fear most will surely come upon you."

"There's always something to take the joy out of living."

"I was fit to be tied."

"Never seen the like of it in all my time."

Acting/Being poor: "They're just putting up the poor mouth."

"They're as poor as Job's turkey."

Going to the outhouse: "I'm going to see a man about a dog."

"I'm going to see Mrs. Jones."

Children's bedtime: "Time to go where the neighbour's dogs won't bark at you."

A bad person: "The worst that ever walked in shoe leather."

Sometimes he'd be home in his office, working on a sermon or studying something, and he'd say: "If *anyone* calls, or comes knocking at the door, I don't want to talk to them or see them.

I've got to get this finished." Someone would say, "What do we tell them, when they see your car in the yard?"

He'd say, "I don't care what you say. Tell them I'm sick in bed—across two chairs, with my feet out through the window, if you want to."

Two others that I remember had unintentional sexual connotations. We were in northern New Brunswick visiting. We were in the Bathurst or Chipman/Minto area and were about to leave to go home. Long trainloads of ore would go through at a certain time of evening and people planned around them, as there was only a level crossing on the road.

The old man asked, very innocently, "What time do the 'Hore' trains go through?" There was shocked silence for a few seconds until they realized what he was asking.

A few minutes later, we were gearing up to go. Everyone was in the kitchen except my mother and the host's wife, who were still in the living room talking. The old man looked around and asked, "Has anyone seen my old quiff?" When everyone looked shocked, thinking he was referring to my mother—he said, "you know—my old quiff hat." The host said, "I should tell you, Reverend, that word you said has a *much* different meaning here."

THE VERY LAST PLACENTIA R.C. CHURCH

Around 2000, Green's Drug Mart at Green's Harbour, with branches in Dildo and Placentia, Newfoundland and Labrador, commissioned replicas of the new Salvation Army Citadel in Green's Harbour and the Roman Catholic Church in Placentia. The design and production were handled by Catherine Karnes Munn (Knob Hill Gallery Inc.) in Fredericton, New Brunswick.

Two batches of each were eventually ordered. The minimum order was 1 gross (144) of an individual replica. A total of 288 of the Roman Catholic Church replicas were available for sale in these stores (two orders of 144). After that, the minimum order went up to 500 of an individual replica, so no more were ordered.

In 2003, I wanted to buy one for my wife, Katie, when I saw them for sale. She did not indicate great interest, so I did not make the purchase. In 2006, she decided she might like to have one. Her mother went looking and was unable to locate one to give her for Christmas that year. There were none left at Green's, and no more were to be ordered.

Not one to take no for an answer, in June 2007 I investigated and discovered that the replica was indeed exclusive to Green's and I visited the three stores in search of one. At the Green's Harbour store (the last store I visited), they found one that

The *very* last Placentia Roman Catholic Church.

a customer had put on layaway and had not returned to pick up, and they sold it to me. The last Placentia R.C. Church in Newfoundland! I gave it to Katie for her birthday.

I thought it might be nice if there was only one more so I could give it to Laurie Shannon, our daughter. I phoned Catherine Karnes Munn in Fredericton and spoke to her husband, Joe Munn. Joe said that they usually tried to keep one of each work in their Archives and since I wanted one so badly, he would go looking for it when he had a chance. He phoned several days later and he had found the *very last one* anywhere. Joe packed it and Catherine addressed and mailed it to me.

The moral of this story: If you really want something badly enough, you can probably get it—especially if you deal with people who really care about their art, and about customer service.

RESPONSE
to
AN ALIEN

Dear Alien:

Thank you for your letter and allow me to clear up some misconceptions. You will need some guidance in understanding humanity and I am pleased to offer my services. Just in what I have written so far, there are a number of things you do not understand:

Alien: To most of Earth's people it means someone like you from another planet or galaxy. To Americans (people who live in the United States of America), it means humans who were not born in America. They divide Aliens into two types:

> *Legal Aliens* have been granted the right to come to America and are allowed to work and live almost as if they were born there.

> *Illegal Aliens*, unfortunately, came without being invited, so they are unable to live openly and work—except to do menial low-paying tasks like gardening and housekeeping for the most rich and powerful Americans. If they cannot find this kind of work, they go to jail or are deported. They really could have simply called them all foreigners, but Americans don't like to alienate people.

Humankind, my Alien friend, is a misnomer. Humans are not kind. Some will kill you just for forgetting to put cheese on their hamburger. Some will kill you because they don't like the colour of your skin. You're safe. You're kind of beige.

In response to your various questions:

Is a hamburger made from ham? No, there isn't any ham in a hamburger.

Why are they called Americans? Good one. Technically, anyone born on either the North or South American continent is American. I guess that "I'm a United States of American" was just too long a sentence. Yet some "Americans" even refer to their country as "These here United States of America." I assume that they do this to avoid confusion in case you guys have a country on some other planet going by the same name.

Why is it not USOA instead of USA? No one knows.

What is this jail where they send an Alien? Another good one. It's a secure place with bars where we put citizens or Aliens who do wrong. From then on, we refer to them as prisoners.

Is it like a cage? Yeah, like a cage they can't get out of, but no, those weren't bad Aliens you saw at the SPCA. Those are pets. We keep a number of lower species in cages.

Are they prisoners? Yeah, they are indeed prisoners. We just *call* them pets—but won't let them go.

Are those little people we saw in cars, prisoners? No. What you saw in cars in those restraining devices are young humans. When pets are with us in cars, they are allowed to stick their head out the window, or sit on the driver's lap, or crawl under the brake pedal.

I hope that I have been of some help in answering your questions. Please write soon.

In sincerity,
Grandpa Pike

PROTECT
THEIR INNOCENCE?

In the spring of 1988 my daughter was five, and I was in my 44th year. I'm not much of a fisherman, but I like to go once in a while. Usually, I don't get the weight of my bait back. I had been around too many women who wouldn't touch a worm. I didn't want my girl to become one of them. I decided I would take Laurie Shannon with me to see what I could teach her.

She peppered me with questions like, "What do fish eat?" I suppose I should have told her that many of them eat smaller fish, and thus prepare her for the real world, but I said that they eat worms and bugs, which is also true. Worms and bugs didn't bother her. She'd just helped me dig up some big juicy ones out behind the henhouse.

"Are worms good for people?" she asked. I probably should have told her that in many parts of the world, people eat worms and bugs and whatever else they can find. I told her that I didn't think they would hurt you, and if she was lost or stranded somewhere they would likely help to keep her alive.

"I'll remember that, Dad," she said, "but I think what I'd probably do is throw the worm in the edge of the water and smash the fish with a big rock when he comes to eat it." You know, it might work. She'd probably catch as many as I have using traditional methods.

We caught one tiny trout, maybe 5 inches long, and she examined it. After a short debate, we decided to throw it back in, and in her words, "let it swim back to its mother." We waited too long. The fish floated belly up downstream and out of her line of vision.

We started packing up to go home, and I changed the subject, as I didn't want to ruin her hopes that the tiny fish would make it back to its mother. I felt bad that she had to see an animal die.

Then she asked me, "Do you think that fish will live, Dad?" I told her that I didn't know, because I didn't want her to cry, although I knew it was as dead as Monty Python's parrot.

"If it doesn't live," I told her, "it will not be wasted as it will make a good meal for some hungry bird or animal."

"That's okay, Dad," she said, "at least it won't be wasted."

A couple of weeks later I spotted a tiny garter snake at home. I picked it up and showed it to her. With little encouragement, she took it, decided it was cute, and then let it go. Snakes, toads, grasshoppers, birds, lady beetles, and caterpillars, she liked them all.

A few days later we were sitting at the picnic table in our yard having a talk and she noticed a spider. A caterpillar was caught in its web and the spider was binding it up securely in threads. She started to cry and, looking up at me, she said, "Look at that mean spider, Dad. I think he's going to eat that pretty caterpillar. Make him let it go, Dad! Make him let it go!"

I could have, as the prey was still alive, but I explained to her instead, that the spider had a right to live too. I told her that they eat mosquitoes, flies, and other insects that bite us and cause disease. I said that there would still be lots of caterpillars left to become butterflies next year.

Slowly her attitude changed, as she studied the spider and the caterpillar. She was intrigued by how the spider gets his meals. We watched him continue to secure his prey until we heard my wife call us in for supper.

I don't remember learning those things when I was five. I'm glad I got a chance to teach her something about the cycle of life. I like to say that everything is just "trying to make a living," so there are no good and bad animals in that sense, but Duke said it just as well when she took my hand to walk inside.

"Everybody has to eat, you know, Dad."

IS SHE FALLING
in
LOVE?

He's a stranger, and he offers her a ride home. They leave an event at the same time. He is, however, a friend of a friend, so she accepts. She gets into the car's passenger front seat with this young guy, just chatting, getting to know each other. It's a cold blustery winter's day out there and she's not dressed for it. She wishes that she had worn something different, something warm, instead of that dress.

He notices her discomfort and turns the heater up. Then he turns the music off so they can talk. He seems nice. They're both rambling on, a mile a minute, trying to find out everything they can about the other. He asks about her—doesn't talk about himself. He likes what he sees and hears. She does too and finds him physically attractive as well.

She shivers, still a bit cold. Then slowly she begins to feel a warm glow right in her core. That warmth spreads up and down and suddenly she's wondering if she's starting to fall in love with this man—a man she hardly knows. Then she realizes that he has simply turned on her seat warmer. Her face reddens.

When they get to her house, he offers to walk her up the driveway. She declines and hurries to her door. He waits until she is safely inside, then pulls away. She wonders will she ever see him again. He didn't ask her out, didn't even ask her contact information.

Then her phone rings. It's him! He already had her number; he got it from the mutual friend. "I didn't want to put you on the spot, but I'd like to take you out to dinner some time. Don't feel obligated in any way." She says yes. Maybe it isn't love, yet, but he did think to turn on the seat warmer for her, didn't he?

CHAPTER 6

ROAD WARRIOR

Many of us who spent much of our lives on the road in sales call ourselves Road Warriors. These stories are of my first job in outside sales, of hotels and restaurants, of merchandising stores, and of course, selling.

They are also about what you surrender—selling your house and moving when you are given a new territory, business terms in common usage and what they *really* mean, and how your age affects your chances of getting a new outside sales job.

The joys of being your own boss, of meeting and exceeding the goals set, and the peace and solitude on those long drives, is equally balanced by the feeling of how much you are missing out on, back home, on those too many nights alone.

Then, every once in a while, something very memorable happens and you happily soldier on.

A LITTLE BIT
of
KINDNESS

I was standing in a *very* long lineup at a Tim's in Riverview, New Brunswick. I placed my order and stood to the side as my friend—who was travelling from Newfoundland with me, moved up to place his. He was a tall, dark, and handsome guy in a three-piece suit.

The crowd was getting restless and we could clearly hear the grumbling and complaining of those waiting in line behind us. Rush hour at Tim's, as many were on their way to work at the mall.

The young lady working the counter looked like she had been there all night without a break—or perhaps she was on her very first shift. She was not what many would term attractive. She seemed nervous and was perspiring heavily. Her hair kept falling in her face. He ordered his coffee as she listened very closely to an accent that was obviously new to her. "Would you like anything else?" she asked.

"No, my love," he told her, and the other two women working at their nearby stations looked up and smiled at him.

She blushed, and grinned as if she had never heard those words before from a good-looking young man. Brushing her hair aside, she kept smiling as she prepared his drink. We left her a nice tip, he took his coffee, and we went to find a table. As we drank, she continued to look in our direction, between customer orders.

My friend and I waved to her, later, as we walked past to exit the store. All three women looked up and smiled at him as we passed by. A little while later, we were at a nearby building supply yard and a quiet knock came at the closed office door where we were presenting our product to the manager.

In walked the young lady from Tim's, her shift over, and said, "Here's your coffee, Dad." She froze for a moment when she saw us, and then smiled. We greeted her and she couldn't stop smiling—especially at my friend.

It *had* been her first shift at the job. Her father asked how it had gone. "Hectic," she told him, "I didn't know if I'd make it through the night. The customers were so grumpy, and then these two guys came along. Be good to them. They were very nice to me." He was.

BUSINESS TERMS
FOR NEWBIES

In my 50 years in the business world, I ran into many terms that often mean something very different from what is actually said. Some people take them literally and are disappointed when the expected action does not ensue. A salesperson who lives by the literal meaning will build a reputation quicker than any other way that I know. It doesn't matter how well you know your product. It isn't important if you are attractive or look good in a suit. But always say what you mean and mean what you say.

"I'll check on that and get right back to you."
Does this mean that they will do so? That depends on your interpretation. If you think it means that they will forget what you said, even while you are saying it, and when you call them a month later, they will say, "I'm still working on that," or "It slipped my mind. I'll get right on it," then you are right. If you think they will, indeed, respond to you in a timely fashion, usually you will be wrong. Anyone who cares about your business, though, will tell you *when* they will get back to you. If they do not have the answer by then, they will contact you and let you know *when* they expect to have it.

"I'll confirm that with you tomorrow."
Some people mean it literally and will get back to you the day after today. Others go by the Mexican meaning. In Spanish, *Mañana* means, literally, tomorrow. It also means "an unspecified future date," as in, "do you want to fix that tractor today?" "No, let's do it manãna." To me, the word tomorrow should mean only *the day after today.*

"Your call is important to us, please stay on the line."
They've left out a few words. What they mean is "If your call was important to us, we would hire a few more people so you don't have to stay on the line until hell freezes over, the Toronto Maple Leafs win a Stanley Cup, or until our Lord and Saviour returns—whichever comes first."

"We'll certainly look at that suggestion."
If you think this means that the company's president, to whom you are speaking, will bring up your great idea on customer service at the next board meeting and the policy will change, then you likely believe Elvis is not dead and the summers are long and hot in Newfoundland. What this really means is, "Our policy is our policy. We have no intention of modifying it, as your suggestion would not improve shareholder value, and might cost us a few pennies that I cannot afford to lose from my paltry million-dollar bonus."

I have always prided myself on doing what I say I will do. If I say I will be at your office on the 23rd at 9 a.m., I will be there early, and patiently wait to see you at 9. If an emergency comes up, I will call and cancel or reschedule, in advance.

I had one dealer in a new territory that must have been used to very sloppy service from the last representative. He marvelled at how I always did what I said I would.

"If you didn't show up, I'd probably look at the obituaries in the Telegram that evening," he told me. We are all made differently and, personally, I lose patience quickly with people whose word is no good. Take every commitment seriously and be tough on yourself and no boss will ever have to.

MAINTAINING YOUR VEHICLE

———————

Having driven about 5 or 6 million kilometres in my work as a commercial traveller, I've learned a few things about vehicle maintenance. Some of the vehicles I drove carried me half a million kilometres and more before I had to trade them in.

I've learned that you don't wait until the oil light comes on before you check the oil. I believe in preventative maintenance, as opposed to waiting for something to give out, and then looking for a place to repair it. If you want to achieve high "mileage," here are two tips that worked for me.

1. Never put your engine under "load" until it is warmed up.

2. Change your oil once a month.

Of course, finding the right place and the right person who will check your car for weaknesses on a regular basis and fix those faults before you get stranded somewhere is just as important. Those kinds of places and people are getting rarer.

What about your other "vehicle"—your body? I smoke, drink, eat greasy foods, and exercise too little. Some days the hardest physical work I did was lift my briefcase or carry my luggage into a hotel. Isn't it odd how we worry more about the condition of a motor vehicle than we do its contents?

I've got 5 million clicks on me too, but my 76-year-old body has not been properly maintained, and my face, from squinting at the sun, is as lined and worn as an old roadmap. Hope I make it to the next checkup! The hardest thing is taking the advice of the doctor—your body's mechanic.

RESTAURANTS

When I'm travelling on business, I like to eat at regular restaurants. Regular as opposed to fast food. You can't get liver and onions, pork chops with applesauce and mashed potatoes, or a real breakfast at a fast-food restaurant.

When I eat, usually sitting alone, I like to read a newspaper while I'm waiting for my food, and continue reading as I eat. If you're sitting alone, there's little else you can do, as there will be no conversation. It's no fun watching other diners when you're eating alone, since you have no one beside you with whom you can make fun of them.

My only real complaint with the regular restaurants is that they usually have three menus: breakfast, lunch, and dinner, each one progressively more expensive. They don't want to serve you $6 bacon and eggs at lunchtime, because the lunch menu starts at $12. They don't want to sell you a $12 grilled cheese sandwich and a bowl of soup at dinner, because the dinner menu starts at $23.

I like bacon and eggs any time of the day. Restaurants use the same grill for everything, so why not give me my bacon and eggs when I want it? I was in a restaurant, about a year ago, at lunch time, and asked if I could get bacon and eggs. No, the girl told me, the breakfast menu stopped at 11 a.m. I decided I would have a sandwich.

"Are these the only sandwiches you have," I asked her, referring to the chicken, ham and cheese, and beef.

"That's all that's on the menu," she told me, "but we can make you any kind you want."

"How about a toasted bacon and egg sandwich?"

"Coming right up, sir," she said with a smile.

So I got my coffee along with my bacon, eggs, and toast, but I wanted the kit that I could put together myself. They won't let you have that. Does that make any sense?

SHOULD YOU MOVE?

After a lifetime of moving from province to province, I've finally come to the conclusion that it is better to stay in one place at almost any cost. We moved some 10 or 12 times when I was growing up, and I have moved about 25 times since then. Since 1977 alone, I have bought and sold nine houses in three provinces. We now live in the tenth.

Why have I moved so much? The first 10 or 12 moves were my father's decision. He was a preacher. As a result of all those moves, I never developed any long-term friendships in my childhood.

My moves as an adult were always for employment. If you are a medical doctor or a lawyer, most often you will join a practice, or set up your own, and stay in the same geographical area for most of your career. In other parts of the work world, it is different. You have to follow the opportunities.

If you choose sales, as I did, and you get into an industry that is rapidly changing and consolidating, you have less choice. If your company fails or is bought out by another and you're not needed, you can either seek an opportunity elsewhere or change careers.

All I wanted to do was sell. I worked in the hardware/building materials and the paint industries. Dozens of companies in that sector have gone out of business. Dozens more have merged with, or been bought out by, other companies, most often with little or no notice. You are working one day, travelling out of the province, and you get the call. A few days later, you meet the new owners and your world changes.

Sometimes they'll tell you right away if you are redundant. Most times, they will not. "There'll be no job losses. It will be business as usual," they say with a big smile. That's when you start looking for another opportunity. Most times I escaped the axe by being proactive and finding something elsewhere.

A few times I have been hired back by the same company when they discovered that they needed me, or could use me. My territories have been variously: Niagara Peninsula, eastern Ontario to Montreal, New Brunswick, the Atlantic Provinces, the Maritimes, Nova Scotia, and Newfoundland, "all of Canada east of Yonge Street," and others.

On balance, I believe it is better to wait it out and find some kind of work in the area where you live. Moving requires you to give up too much. You lose touch with friends. You lose contact with all the other people you knew and the changes taking place in your hometown. Your kids have to switch schools. You lose on real estate fees each time you sell a house. You lose a place called home.

If you have to move to stay employed, visit home often, at least once a year, and see everyone you can while you are there. If you don't, and then you decide to move back later or retire there, you'll find out that you are a stranger. Essentially, you will find that you have no home. It vanished while you were gone. That's what has happened to me. It's a sad and regrettable thing.

TOO
OLD?

I couldn't find a job! After over 50 successful years in the work-force in sales, business development, franchise development, and retail banner support, I couldn't find a job.

For most of those years I'd travelled in Ontario and Atlantic Canada, working for national and international companies—growing sales and market share and accumulating an enviable list of successes.

Working with paint, hardware, and building material manufacturers and distributors, I've met targets, exceeded expectations, won salesperson of the year awards, and logged about 5 or 6 million kilometres by car. In addition to that, I successfully managed two of my own businesses—a sales agency and a retail store.

Those millions of kilometres—just *to get to* work. Most weeks I averaged 2,500 kilometres and 70 to 80 hours, counting driving time, meetings with clients, paperwork, and computer work in the evenings. I have spent more nights in hotel and motel rooms than I have at home. Let's not talk about the days and nights storm-stayed in remote areas, the waiting at airports, and the hours on planes.

I rarely took a vacation. Anything more than a long weekend

meant boredom. So now, apparently, I had become too old. I didn't believe it.

I thought that I could do another million or so kilometres, open new accounts, grow existing ones, and sign dealers into retail programs. In fact, I knew I could *still* do those things and an overwhelming majority of the clients I've worked with would agree.

It is illegal to discriminate against anyone solely on the basis of age, of course. The discrimination can be subtle, as in "This company is looking for a recent graduate" or "Ideal *entry level* position." A 50-year-old recent graduate need not apply in the first instance, and any older person will not get an interview in the second.

Although I was eminently qualified for the jobs I pursued, I couldn't get to a face-to-face interview. In a Skype interview, my grey hair and weathered face betray me. Most often I was being screened by a junior HR person, and although the interview seemed to go great, I'd never get to a face-to-face interview. In a telephone interview, they simply add up the years that show on your résumé and ask who else you've worked for.

Most headhunters and employment agencies rely heavily on the Internet to check you out. They search you on Facebook, LinkedIn, and other social media and Google your name. They won't find anything bad, but they'll find my age and see my face.

That's enough for many people in their 20s and 30s—the ones that are doing the hiring now—to conclude that I was a dinosaur.

I had one face-to-face interview with a company which, apparently, didn't do that homework. After reviewing my résumé and two telephone interviews, they were clearly excited that I was exactly what they needed.

I was invited to an interview at a hotel. According to the lady on the front desk, whom I knew, they were meeting only two people, me before lunch and another person after lunch.

When the two young guys answered the meeting room door, their smiles faded and their faces fell. The interview that was scheduled for an hour, followed by lunch, lasted a bare 20 minutes.

They told me about all the travel—the early mornings and late nights, and how hard that part of the job was. It was clear that they wanted a younger guy, and they forgot all the good that they had heard about me—after they read my face. I tried to stay positive but escaped without all of my dignity intact.

So why don't employers want to hire older people? Here is some of their reasoning, I believe.

(My responses in italics.)

1. "Is the old dude/lady able to get out of bed in the morning?"
   "Yes, I will be halfway to my first call before the young guy is even out of bed."

2. "Is he/she applying only because they need the money?"
   "No. I am driven. There's only one thing that I would rather do than work and that only takes a few minutes."

3. "Will he forget what he is supposed to do, right after we tell him?"
   "No."

4. "What if he/she has a heart attack?"
   "What if a younger person has a heart attack or gets cancer or diabetes or just quits because he didn't know how hard the job is?"

5. "Can she/he keep up with the competition?"

    "Yes! I have developed the relationships and the reputation that will open doors. I welcome long full days. I will outperform the young guy who needs to get home at night because he has a young family waiting."

I also had great references, from industry leaders—people who knew me well, because I'd worked with or for them—all to no avail. References are rarely checked until the decision to hire is made.

Most hirings are done by formula today. The computer program counts how many keywords and action words are used in the resume. They are looking for the perfect person who fits an artificial profile. A robot. I believe that the key indicator of how an employee will perform is how they have performed at *previous* jobs. In sales, it is all about building relationships and, subsequently, trust. A robot might get to your head but it won't get to your heart. You need to do both to succeed in sales.

I was too old. They were telling me that in so many ways, but they wouldn't tell me directly, which indicates that at the very least they knew I wasn't stupid. We both know that it is illegal to exclude someone based on age. A job will come, I believed, and the new employer will wonder how they made out without me!

It didn't, so at age 70 I started a new career: writing. Too old? Hell, no!

WHO
ARE THEY THERE
TO SERVE?

I've never liked those high-rise hotels. I've always chosen, where possible, a motel, preferably with a drive-up unit. Unless you've been in a building where the lower floor was burning (I have), you may not understand the fear. So when I started on the road in the early 1970s, I stayed at numerous small motels. If they didn't have a restaurant, no problem. I had a hibachi and charcoal in the trunk. I'd cook my own supper, sitting in a folding lawn chair while drinking a beer.

Often other commercial travellers stayed at the same motel and we'd get together to cook our supper and sip a few cold ones. Later on, the guitars would come out. But after Labour Day or by Thanksgiving, these places would often close until spring. They'd be packed during the summer with tourists, and often they'd "lose" your reservation if a bus tour or other large group showed up unexpectedly.

So I got to thinking, who are they there to serve? Tourists, obviously. I started becoming more selective with where I'd stay. I still do not support any motel or restaurant that stays open only seasonally. At the time that I was in the hardware/building supply industry, it's safe to say that all of the stores I called on lost money during the winter months. None of them closed during the winter.

When I moved from Nova Scotia to a small village in New Brunswick, it was a few days before I got a fridge and stove set up and working right. There was a small motel/restaurant/gift shop just down the road. I decided I would go there for a few meals in the meantime. The first time I pulled in, the clerk noticed my licence plate and asked if I was visiting from Nova Scotia.

I told her that I had just moved to their village and introduced myself. Her smile faded and she was really slow in coming over to serve me, although there was only one other party there. It was clear, right from the start, that she was assuming no gift shop sales, no room, and only the occasional meal. She decided she didn't need customers like that.

I went back the next day and I was, essentially, ignored. It took me the best part of an hour to get a grilled cheese sandwich and a bowl of soup. I was barely finished when she approached me and asked if I would be much longer. They had a group coming in a half hour and they needed my table. I paid and left without drinking my coffee.

I lived there for 10 years and *never* entered the business again. All those Christmases, Valentine's Days, and other special occasions when my wife and I would have patronized them, we didn't, all because this clerk (owner!) was interested only in tourists.

There was a motel in another small New Brunswick community where I stayed regularly. I'd be there two or three nights a week every third week. They blocked the room for three nights in case I needed it. I came back about supper time one evening on the third night and my suitcase had been packed and set by the room door. My key would not unlock the door.

I went to the front desk and they told me that they had rented the room and none other was available. I spoke to the manager (owner), who defended their new policy with, "you should have told us when you checked in whether it was for two or three nights." "Thank you," I told her, paid for the two nights, and drove across the river to another motel. Over the next 20 or so years they lost, by my estimation, between 620 and 960 room nights from me. And this was a motel that struggled to break even in the wintertime.

Curiously, I received a Christmas card from them every year for 10 years or so after that which read, simply, "Merry Christmas." Never a note saying "hope to see you soon" or "sorry about your last stay," just the card with their name rubber-stamped at the bottom. Hey, same to you! If it wasn't for you, I would not have found a place that appreciated a customer who would help pay the lights and heat during those long cold winter months—and never ever checked me out when my clothes and other belongings were still in the room.

So, if you're in the food and beverage or lodging business in a town which I visit, and you're only after tourist dollars, I won't darken your door. I'll leave any spare space you have inside for your preferred customers and choose a competitor that is there to serve my needs, year-round.

WORKING HARD
or
HARDLY WORKING?

It doesn't take any prodding to get out of bed in the morning to go to work, if you love what you do. You set your alarm as a backup, but you're up and gone before it even rings. You forget to eat, don't need breaks, and 16- or 18-hour workdays aren't work at all.

A long-haul trucker once told me there were times when he was so tired that he'd forget where he was going. He would pull over, open the back of his trailer, and look at the freight and the waybills in order to remember—and he loved his job. I never understood that until I took a job in outside sales.

As a commercial traveller, I regularly worked this way, many days driving 600 or 800 kilometres. In the car at 5 a.m., making calls until 8 p.m., and finally into a hotel at night, on my laptop, returning emails, doing reports, or working on business plans, presentations, and budgets for dealers, until midnight.

In a different bed, in a different town, and often in a different province each night. Sometimes I woke up at 2 or 3 a.m. in a dark hotel room and had to go look out the window to remember where I was. Fifty years of it.

Now, I don't travel at all. We just moved back to Newfoundland. My wife has a job that she loves. She manages a building supply centre and furniture store. She is up before daybreak.

She goes down the driveway, out around a mountain, past the ocean and vistas worthy of a hundred postcards onto the flats of Placentia, that historic community which 350 years ago was Plaisance, France's capital in the New World.

She drives past her store, past her twin sister's house, waves to her, and goes over to her mother's house for morning coffee. She will be home after 5:30 and sometime before 9:30 p.m. She has not been able to do these things in her hometown for over 30 years. It is now her turn.

Now that the addition to the house we bought is completed, and the interior redone, I am concentrating on my other obsession—writing. Still, I'd give anything to be back on the road working. Some feel bad for their spouses who have to work so hard to make a go of it. I'm happy for mine, but I have to admit, I'm a little envious.

MERCHANDISING
OUT AROUND
THE BAY

I've been through at least 100 store merchandisings in my years on the road. I don't remember even one where the store plan didn't have to be adjusted. Sometimes it was minor, like a small product category missing. In that case, you took a hard look at any other category that could be condensed, and adjusted the plan accordingly. Other times it was major, like an upright support post shown in the wrong place or storefront windows shown as a bare wall that could be used. In that case, you had to rework the whole plan.

Sometimes the merchandisers showed up but the store fixtures or the opening order didn't. Other times, vice versa. Rarely did one of these jobs go smoothly. An empty building is a piece of cake compared to trying to merchandise an existing store which remains open during the transition.

What initially appeared to be a very difficult one became one of the easiest in outport Newfoundland. It was an existing store and was to remain open during the remerchandising process. The first run of fixtures needed to move over 2 feet to widen the main drive aisle. Then the subsequent rows of fixtures had to be moved over 1 foot each so that the aisles were all wide enough. But the shelves were loaded with existing inventory!

Normally, we would strip the first fixture of product, put it in shopping carts, and then dissemble and reassemble that run of fixtures in its new position. (You can't just push the empty fixtures to their new position and destroy the flooring.) But the store had only two shopping carts and there wasn't another store for miles where we could borrow them.

We explained the problem to the owner; he said, "No problem, b'ys, just give me a minute. I'll be right back." A few minutes later he was back with a piece of 2x4, a crowbar, a knife, and a bag with something in it. He laid the 2x4 next to the end post and then took a big soggy piece of fatback out of the bag and sliced off a 2-inch-square piece.

Buddy and I glanced at each other as if to say "this man's crazy," but it turned out that he wasn't. He took the crowbar in one hand, laid it over the 2x4 right next to the post, and, using the wood as a fulcrum, stood on the crowbar. That post lifted from the floor. Then he handed me the piece of pork to slip under the post, fat-side-down, and when it was in place, he lowered the post back down.

We did that with each post on the 16-foot run of fixtures. Then he called a few of his employees over and five of us *slid* the fixture to the required distance. When it was placed exactly right, we had only to lift each post and remove the pork. The floor was greasy but undamaged.

We actually saved time on the job by not having to empty and tear down each run of shelving. Sometimes you need neither an engineer nor a long row of shopping carts—just everyday ingenuity.

CREST
HARDWARE

The hardware wholesaler founded in 1849—earlier known as Wood, Alexander and James, and later simply as Wood Alexander Ltd.—operated out of a four-storey warehouse in Hamilton. It was the start of the 1970s when I worked from that antiquated multi-windowed (many of them broken) building. I got my first cat, a frequent visitor on hunting expeditions at night, from that building—but that's another story.

Product was stocked, picked for dealer orders, and moved up and down a rickety cramped wooden elevator. Although their time had passed, buggy whips and blacksmith's anvils, along with 35,000 or 40,000 other items for sale, were available for sale to hardware stores. I was hired as an outside salesman, so I worked inside for only a few days, as orientation.

Our franchise program and banner were known as Crest Hardware and this was the first such chain in the hardware business in Canada. We had about 200 Crest stores in Ontario and a few in the Eastern Townships of Quebec. At the time, Pro, Home, and Dominion Hardware were also active in Canada. Our company was owned by Gambles out of the US, and the Canadian subsidiary was known as Gamble-Macleods. As well as Crest Hardware, the Canadian company also operated the Stedman's

Department Store group and a chain of hardware stores in Western Canada called Macleod's.

The Canadian company later went through some changes, and eventually what was left of it morphed into Cotter Canada, which continued to operate Stedman's and MacLeod's stores for some time.

Cotter became Tru-Serv Canada and was acquired by Rona Inc. Rona, in turn, was sold to Lowe's. Crest Hardware, however, is no more.

I was with Wood-Alex and Crest for several years, but, in my opinion, we were "starved" out of business by head office. The other banners, like Home and Dominion, were developing more sophisticated marketing and advertising programs for their members and we were not, and quickly falling behind the times. The other groups were beginning to use data entry units for placing orders.

Their catalogues were on microfiche, updated monthly with product and price changes. We had only a paper catalogue and no computer. Head office continued to drag its feet on investing money, while our competitors leapfrogged ahead of each other. By 1975, they were already in a whole different pond, and too far ahead to catch.

Imagine our competitors' dealers keying in and transmitting their own orders and having them shipped the next day. Contrast that with our dealers, writing the quantities they wanted on the pages of the catalogue, tearing those pages out and mailing them in to be filled and shipped. Replacement pages came back along with the order—that's how the catalogue was kept updated. Dealers would forget to insert the new pages, or they would be lost in transit sometimes, and soon the catalogue was ragged and incomplete.

I kept my copy of the catalogue, the 75th edition, when I left the company. I weighed it this morning: 11.5 pounds. On each page are product illustrations, pricing, and a column to enter quantities and the dealer's name.

Keep in mind that if the dealer needed to look up anything on any of the pages involved after he/she had mailed their order, they had no access to them until the order and the replacement pages (hopefully) came in.

So if they had ordered 300 items on 300 different pages that week, they had a much skinnier catalogue. Our customer service/order desk people went crazy, without a computer or even a fax, trying to pass information verbally to dealers who needed it immediately—often information that the dealers had mailed in on those missing pages.

Most of our stores were small, 2,000 square feet or less. This was in the day before home centres or even many building-supply stores. Building supplies—lumber, plywood, etc.—were sold in lumberyards. Most lumber yards sold a few nails and hammers but not much else in hardware.

The American company which owned us also sold appliances—fridges, stoves, and freezers. (We called them "White Goods" then.) Appliances were a big part of department stores' business in the US. Stores like Gambles and Sears did well with them. Our little stores were not big enough to stock much, if any, of this product category. Still, we kept getting pushed to focus on them more. In addition to the space problem, our dealer pricing made it nearly impossible for our dealers to make any money on the sale.

Our store design or store planning department was a farce. It took months to get even a blueprint for a new layout. I started doing my own. From past experience in the food business, I had basic knowledge.

I read books and magazines to get ideas and studied the merchandising in our competitors' stores. Then I found a business which sold supplies for architects and made blueprints. Somehow, I managed to produce some very workable plans.

Anything was better than what then existed in some of our stores—unadjustable wooden fixtures, and, for pegboard, 4-inch finishing nails were driven into plywood to hold the new products in blister packs that were designed to be hung. Almost a third of Crest's sales now came from one territory—mine. I knew it couldn't last. The company, I mean.

With all the sales management, merchandising, marketing, and other supposed professionals working inside, who should be on top of things, it is usually the outside salespeople (the road warriors) who first recognize major problems.

I knew what the dealers wanted. I knew what was available elsewhere. Give them exactly what they want and need, and you will be successful. (The challenge is in finding a way to make money doing it.) I tired eventually of beating my head against a brick wall, trying to get changes. Finally, in 1975, I decided that I would leave and go back east to live.

I wrote a letter to Walter Hackborn, then president of Home Hardware, to see if they could use anyone in the Atlantic. They had Walter Aylward, who travelled the whole region for them; they needed no one else. I heard that Dominion Hardware was considering expanding their territory to the Atlantic. They would need good people. I applied, was hired, and later that year signed my first of many Dominion Hardware Stores in the Atlantic provinces.

In the next few years, Crest managed to develop a new trade style and logo, opened a modern distribution centre in Burlington, Ontario, and tried, but failed, to revitalize their program. Too little, too late. The new centre was hardly up and running when the company went down for the count.

At my first sales meeting with Dominion, the sales manager asked what my title had been at Crest. I told them it was Zone Manager. Someone mumbled "Twilight Zone," and everyone laughed. It hurt, as I had done all that I, as an individual, could do to try to keep that company alive, and I still believed it could have been saved. I got over it, as no insult was meant to me personally. It's hard to watch something die, though, that you knew how to save but didn't have the authority or the resources with which to do it.

I did get a good laugh, however, at the last Crest sales meeting which I attended before going east. It was in the summer of 1975. I had, just six months earlier, accepted a transfer from Hamilton to Belleville, Ontario, with Crest. My territory was from Oshawa, to Montreal, and north to Smith's Falls. As I'd been boarding with a family, I had no furniture, only my clothes, a few boxes of books and files, an old record player, and a dozen Bob Dylan records.

I rented an apartment. The small second-storey walk-up was fully furnished, except for a TV. At sales meetings, I sat next to Gord English. Gord was constantly buying and selling stuff, some of which he kept in the trunk of his company car. If Gord didn't have it, he could get it, at a bargain price. I had bought a used TV from him for $25.

At that last sales meeting, Mr. Lord, the sales manager, was droning on and on about "White Goods"—selling more and getting better margins on these durable and semi-durable products.

Most of the guys were staring at Lord with glazed eyes reddened by hangovers. Gord and I, however, were talking about the TV I'd bought from him. Suddenly Lord said, in a sarcastic

HOME OF

Crest

STORES

LAURIE PIKE
ZONE MANAGER

(416) 522-1371
P.O. BOX 480, HAMILTON, ONT.
RESIDENCE (613) 962-4101
106½B STATION ST., BELLEVILLE, ONT.

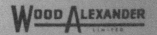

tone, "English and Pike, do you have some thoughts on the matter that you'd like to share with the group?"

Gord froze, but Pike spoke up. "Yeah, as a matter of fact I think we do. I bought a TV set from Gord two weeks ago. When I plugged it in, it worked fine. Two minutes later it made a crackling sound and went dead. I've tried everything but it's dead as a doornail. We were trying to determine if you would consider that a durable or a semi-durable."

The salesmen, knowing Gord's reputation, broke out laughing but Mr. Lord didn't crack a smile, and resumed imparting his wisdom on durables and semi-durables ad nauseam. (Names disguised or eliminated to protect the guilty.)

RIP Crest Hardware.

ON THE WRONG SIDE
of
SELLING DOORS

For several years, while travelling in sales, I sold doors and mouldings exclusively. I watched them being made in the factory and learned a lot about doors. One is that a hollow core door is called that for a very good reason: it is hollow.

There is only a narrow wooden frame, perhaps 2 inches wide around the perimeter of the frame and across the middle, and a larger block of wood where the lockset/door handle will be. The rest of the interior is simply air. When painting one of these doors, I also learned that you need to paint all six sides—that means top and bottom, and both edges, not just the panels (the faces of the door). The reason is moisture.

If any part is not sealed, it will breathe and either absorb or expel moisture, often causing the door to warp. We carried a little pocket mirror to look at the top and bottom of an installed warped door to verify if it had been painted.

I went to look at a complaint where the customer had trimmed a door at the bottom to fit. It was a 6-foot 8-inch-high door that had been trimmed at the bottom to make it fit a 6-foot 6-inch opening. He had taken the whole 2-inch difference off the bottom of the door! The panels had started to curve inward at the bottom. This visit was at 10 a.m., and the customer was already drunk. I started to explain, but the customer didn't want any exaplanations. The door was defective and he wanted a new one. The other three men playing cards at the kitchen table, all intoxicated, chiming in with their condemnation, didn't help any.

Deciding that discretion is the better part of valour, I chose to agree with him. It was only one door. I was about to leave the company anyway. "Defective as hell," I told them, "I'll have a new one sent over." I sent a 6-foot 6-inch door to him, and do you know what he did? He sawed 2 inches off the bottom again, without measuring first! By now, though, I had left the territory and the new guy had to deal with him, thanks be to Jesus.

At that time, there was a shortage of doors in the southern US. The office got a call one day from a small distributer in Tennessee, I believe it was. We checked out the shipping costs and quoted them a price based on several truckloads.

Buddy called back after they arrived. They were all too short! We had, inadvertently, shipped truckloads of 6-foot 6-inch-high doors to him! The standard in North America was 6 feet 8 inches. We stocked both heights because the standard in Newfoundland and Labrador had been 6 feet 6 inches, and there were a lot of renovations going on. It's much easier to replace just the door than tearing out the door frame, doing the carpentry, and replacing with a higher door.

We took the doors back, of course, as it was our mistake— and they were resold in Newfoundland. But I remember that complaint, because the American customer used a word I'd never heard before. He said, "They could be used, I suppose, but to make them tight, it would take one *bodacious* amount of weatherstrip!"

CHAPTER 7

BITTERSWEET TIMES

It's strange how some things can make you happy, but still a little sad at the same time. It could have been a missed opportunity to find out more about somebody. It could be learning something after an event occurred and after you've walked away and now wishing you'd asked more questions. Or maybe you'd like to relive the event because you missed saying or doing one little thing which might have led to a different ending. The answer often is the words were said—but you both needed the ability to read between the lines to hear them.

A STRANGER
at
THE DOOR

_____

We weren't long living on Taylor's Hill in Hillsborough, New Brunswick, in 2008 when, one day, the doorbell rang. We'd had very little company and weren't expecting any that day. My wife got up quickly to answer and I wasn't far behind her. When she opened the door a neatly dressed older man was standing there with a bouquet of flowers.

He asked her, "Is this where Laurie Shannon lives?" My first thought was, who is this old skeet that's trying to hit on my daughter? She wasn't long out of Dalhousie University with a BScN and had begun working as an RN at Moncton Hospital. Laurie Shannon lived with us but had the mother-in-law suite situated at the other end, with its own entrance.

Katie explained the latter to him and told him that she was not home. He looked disappointed. She asked if there was anything we could do. He handed her the flowers and explained. His wife had been Laurie Shannon's patient. She looked after her for the last few months. His wife had just passed away.

He had come here with the flowers to thank Laurie Shannon for the considerate care she had given his wife. Katie told him that we would give her the flowers and pass on his kind words.

That was the day I knew that our daughter had chosen the

right career path. Since then, she has moved to the US, working as a travel nurse at some of the places hardest hit by COVID-19—places like McAllen, Texas, on the Mexican border, and Gallup, New Mexico, on the Navajo Nation reserve. Am I proud of her? I s'pose I am!

LAURIE SHANNON MARRIED THE SAME MAN TWICE!

_____

The perfect wedding! That's the stuff of which many young women's dreams are made. From picking the date, to finding the venue, to selecting a gown, to choosing bridesmaids and their dresses, the guest list, the invitations, the flowers, and perhaps even a wedding planner and a videographer, no detail escapes them.

It was a bright sunny summer's day in 2009 when family and friends from all over the Atlantic provinces converged on our property on Taylor's Hill in Hillsborough, New Brunswick. The wedding was held outdoors. Our wonderful next-door neighbours, Barb and Hugh Morrisey, pitched in to help. The house was fully decorated inside and out. All those chairs and long tables which the Morriseys found and delivered were set up, inside, for the feast after the wedding. Relatives who arrived early helped.

It was a wonderful time that I will remember forever. I have 100 or so pictures of that special day. Duke and Vic had previously moved into what is known as a mother-in-law suite in our house. They were going to stay!

It was as perfect a wedding as one could ask for. So, you may be asking yourself, "Why would Duke marry him again, when this wedding went so perfectly?" Well, I've just described their second wedding. Let me explain why the first one wasn't good enough.

Duke and Vic met online before she graduated from Dalhousie University in 2007 with a BScN degree. She went to work at the Moncton Hospital.

They conversed online for some time and then by phone— he from his home in Lewisburg, Tennessee, and she from her apartment in Moncton. Then they decided to live together, and Vic moved to Canada. As an American citizen with only a passport, he was required to leave Canada before the end of six months or be considered an illegal alien. After almost six months, they went by car back to the US border. Vic went across, came back, had his documents stamped, and all went well. Now he could stay for up to another six months.

So, at approximately the end of 12 months, they decided to go to the border so that he could repeat the process. It's a good run from Moncton to the nearest border crossing at St. Stephen, New Brunswick / Calais, Maine. They arrived there on December 9, 2008, in a blizzard.

Duke parked on the Canadian side and waited for Vic to walk across and then return with his stamped passport. The minutes grew to an hour and by now Duke was getting frantic. She started to cross to the American side in her car, and as she was on the bridge separating the two countries, she saw Vic being escorted to the American side by two armed guards.

When she got over and pulled up to the window, she was questioned about the purpose of her visit. Pointing to Vic, she said, "that's my fiancé. I don't know what is going on." They let her go into the building but kept her car keys, as they were going to search the car. Inside the building, she saw Vic. He had been refused re-entry to Canada because he had overstayed his six months by a few days. The Americans questioned both Vic and

Duke and finally told them that they were free to go and gave Duke back her car keys. Vic could *still* not leave the USA! If he tried, he would be arrested on the Canadian side.

With their limited funds, they decided to get a motel room, stay overnight, and try to devise a plan. There they talked and cried and then talked some more. Duke decided to call Immigration at the Canadian border, for one last try. She got through to a nasty female officer who told her, "No way. The only way he's getting back in is if you are married." She laughed and hung up.

Duke told Vic what the woman had said, and then she added, "Why don't we?" Vic said yes and called his mother to advise her! Duke ran to the front desk, and explained their dilemma to the two young ladies. They let her use a laptop. She found out that the "30-day wait period" legislation had been eliminated. If they could get married, then they could go right across after getting the official documents.

First, they needed a marriage licence. The only trouble was that the town hall in Calais closed in 30 minutes! They got there 15 minutes before closing. They found a kind and understanding official, a Justice of the Peace. Her name was Theresa Porter.

Despite both Duke and Vic being named after their fathers, sharing the same birthday, and several other coincidences, she overcame any suspicion she may have had and issued them a marriage licence. It was after 5 p.m., closing time. Duke told her, "All we need now is to find someone who could marry us." Theresa Porter's face lit up and she said, "I can do that!"

She stopped two women who were leaving work and asked them to stay as she had a special ceremony to perform and needed witnesses. The women agreed. Then this lady totalled up the costs of the licence and marriage ceremony.

Duke knew she had enough in the bank to pay, but her card was declined. The lady said sometimes this happened with Canadian cards. The bank was closed.

Then this angel called the bank across the street and spoke to the manager, who was still there, to explain the situation. The manager met Duke on the steps and let her in. "Big Day," he told her as she withdrew her money.

The lady at the town hall waited at their locked front door and let Duke, covered in snow, back in. They went back to her office, where Duke remembered that she had not called her mother and me to let us know. She made the call. Meanwhile Vic, who can be quite charming, was entertaining the Justice of the Peace and the witnesses. They were handed a standard wedding vow and both accepted it. Duke was in ripped jeans, and Vic sported a Metallica T-shirt.

Everyone cried and then when they got to the "With this ring I thee wed" part, they all laughed, as there were no rings. Then came hugs all around and the JP (Ms. Porter) gave Duke her card with her personal cell number on the back in case anyone doubted their documents at the border. (Duke kept that card in her wallet for years, until it finally disintegrated.)

They then rushed back to the motel to pick up their belongings. The girls at the motel were delighted to have played a part in what could have been a scene in a romance movie. They refunded their money—calling it a wedding gift.

At 6 p.m., they arrived back at the border. After having the documents scrutinized and while waiting for the car to be searched again, Duke walked over to the Canadian side and dealt with an unfriendly guard who couldn't believe that it was a marriage certificate—not just a marriage licence that she was being handed.

She wanted to know who married them. Duke pulled out the card from the JP and pointed out her cell number on the back.

She insisted that Duke go get Vic and come back in. Back across the bridge—cold and wet, retelling the whole story, and finally getting her car keys back. At the Canadian side, they wanted the keys to search the car again. They had to fill out more documents, and then Duke and Vic were taken to separate rooms and interrogated—once again. Apparently, their answers matched and Vic was handed his document so that he could cross back to Canada.

Duke says the car was running on empty but they wanted to get out of town so badly that she wouldn't stop for gas until they were well out of St. Stephen. She has fond memories of the Americans with whom she dealt. Not so the Canadian authorities.

So—now you know why my Onliest Baby Girl married the same man twice.

THE CLASSY LADY
in the
NASH METROPOLITAN

I hadn't thought about her in 40 years, I s'pose. Then I saw a picture of a little turquoise and white Nash Metropolitan on the Internet, and it all came back to me. The last time I saw her was in 1964 when I was working at an IGA grocery store in the south end of Halifax.

I was a clerk there, 21 years old, and filled shelves, packed grocery at the front end, and took orders to customers' cars. We were allowed to accept tips, after saying "no need to do that," or some such words, when offered one. We were not to look or act like we expected one. It was part of our service. A few, mostly older, people tipped—especially if it was a big order, or if they were walking and you had to take a cart to their nearby residence. On a busy day, you might end up with 50 cents, which you could splurge on with a few draft beers on your way home, if you didn't need groceries.

The lady in the Metropolitan didn't park in our lot, but across the street at the curb. I suspect that she wanted to avoid having careless drivers open their doors into her vehicle. If memory serves, it was either late on a Thursday or Friday morning that this classy lady did her weekly shopping. She was slim. She was pretty. She was always perfectly groomed and dressed like she owned a womenswear store. She was married. Her rings told me that, and the cashiers called her Mrs. She was also one of the kindest people I'd ever met. She was older, though, probably about 40 (40 was old then). I was young and single and saw her only as a classy lady.

She always tipped me, always asked how my job was going, talked to me about news and current events, and asked me about my future plans. Some of the guys I worked with used to kid me about her—"Hey, Pike, your girlfriend just came in." I always packed her groceries and took them to her car. First, I'd open her door for her and then close it once she was behind the wheel. Next, she'd hand me the key to the trunk, if she wanted the order there. If it was just a small amount, she'd ask me to put it in the passenger side. She tipped me every time.

I could tell by her bearing, manners, and her articulation that she was a well-educated woman and undoubtedly well-to-do. She probably lived in one of those fancy mansions further down in the south end. I never found out where she lived.

If she saw where and how I lived, outside of work, she would have been shocked. After paying for my room out of my $30 or so weekly salary, I had enough left to buy canned pea soup, heated on my hotplate, and bread and margarine to go with it. Later, when my culinary skills improved, I learned to make Kraft Dinner. There were no escargot, imported cheeses, and British marmalade in my weekly groceries.

She always talked about me, not her. She knew my career goals, because she asked. I told her that I planned to move to Ontario and go to work for a big supermarket chain, work my way up to manager, and then go out on the road in sales, probably with a food manufacturer.

I didn't tell her that I had given my notice until the final week that I was there. She touched me on the arm and said, "No!" Then she asked for her tip back—and gave me a $10 bill. I started to object. I swear to God that a tear came to her eye, and she said, "but I want to, Laurie." I took it, and she wished me well.

In Ontario, I went to work for Food City and worked my way up to assistant manager. One more notch (store manager) and then I would look for a job in outside sales. I didn't get back to Halifax for several years, but when I did, I drove to the old IGA store on both Thursday and Friday mornings to see if she would show up. I parked near the entrance because I thought she may have a different car by now—but I would recognize her—coming or going. I had it all planned. I'd wait until I saw her leave and then hurry over and say, "May I help you to your car with this?" She didn't show up.

If she's still alive, then she is probably close to 100 years old by now. I've long since forgotten her name, but if I knew it, I'd go on the Internet and try to trace her. Oh well, maybe some older person in the Halifax area will read this story and remember or know a real classy lady, from the south end, who drove a turquoise and white Nash Metropolitan back in 1964. I'd like to know how the rest of her life went/is going. We didn't talk about her, back then. I wish we had.

THE BEST PART
ABOUT WRITING

It's not the endless hours at the computer. It's not seeing your name as author on a book cover—and it's definitely not staring at a blank page, trying to find a way to make the reader feel what you want to say. The best part, for me, is the book signing.

Here you get a chance to meet people who have read your book or are about to pick up a copy of your latest book. You meet the famous and celebrated too—premiers, MPs, mayors, artists, musicians, and more. And you meet ordinary people, people who look up to you because you are a published writer. An author.

Often you meet people who also write, and you can relate to them. When I personalize a book for someone like that, I try to encourage them by writing something like this: "Best wishes for success with your own writing. Keep writing!" Then you get someone—when there is a lineup for signings—who lets you explain for five minutes what your book is about before they tell you that they are not buying today, but they wonder if you know a shortcut to their getting their own book published.

Sometimes you connect with people in a special way. A year or so ago, I was at a Costco signing when a group of three or four came to the table to speak to me. They were Pikes—a fairly common name in Newfoundland and Labrador—but no relation to me. One of the ladies said that her dad always went by the name Grandpa Pike, not Poppy or Grampy. He had my book *Grandpa Pike's Outhouse Reader*, loved it, and jokingly claimed it was *his*. He had recently died and they buried it with him.

Most times it's fun and you should never prejudge a prospect who stops by. I was doing a signing once at a busy drugstore. One of the staff was standing near the end of the counter where my little table was set up, and she was pointing out this signing promotion to waiting customers.

A scruffy looking young man with long hair and multiple tattoos, who looked like he had been sleeping in his car for the last two weeks, was next in line. He had a bottle of shampoo in his hand, and I couldn't help thinking, "He really needs that." He glanced at my book and said, "That looks interesting. I'll come back for one later." I thanked him.

He was the last in that wave of customers and when he was out the door, I said to the lady who was assisting me, with a laugh, "Wanna bet on whether he'll come back?" "No," she told me, "he will be back. He buys books here all the time. He's an undercover RCMP officer, and it looks like he was up all night in a stakeout."

MY FATHER'S WATCH

We were never close. We didn't see eye to eye on many things. That relationship deteriorated even more when he divorced my mother and married a woman only a few years older than me, when I was still in high school.

As an adult, I visited him a few times, but there was no closeness, although I think he tried. He died in 1990, when I was 46 and he was 83. I went to his funeral in Amherst, Nova Scotia, where he had been living at the time. About a month or so later, I went to see his wife. I was interested in getting a few books from his large library, and anything else she had, would part with, and which I could keep and pass on to my daughter.

She went into another room for a few minutes and came out with a tiny cardboard box. It would have been his jewelry box where he kept armbands, cuff links (he called them studs), and watches. She told me that everything else was gone. I couldn't get a straight answer from her on what she had sold, given away, or sent to the dump.

She took out of the box two odd cufflinks and handed them to me. "You may as well have these," she said. "They're not worth anything." I took them and noticed that the only other thing in the box was an old watch. "Can I see that?" I asked. She handed it to me and said, "you may as well take that too. It doesn't work."

I remembered that old Bulova watch! It was the one he'd worn in the 1950s and 1960s, given to him by the church congregation in 1948 when we moved from Newfoundland to Canada. I took it, of course, thanked her, and left. I haven't seen or heard of her since.

I couldn't get the watch to work, as it had been wound too tight and something had locked or broken inside. About 10 years later, I decided to take it to a jeweller to see if it could be fixed. After asking around, I was told that the best place was Grand Time at the Murray Premises in downtown St. John's. The owner, Barry Strickland, who worked only on Swiss movement watches and was trained in Switzerland, operated the business along with his wife and partner, Rachel, whom he had met while training in Switzerland.

He cleaned it and found parts to replace the worn or broken ones. I wanted my father's name and dates on the back, along with mine, my daughter Laurie Shannon's, and space for one more name, when Laurie decided to whom she would leave it. It was a lot of engraving in a very small space, but Barry found an expert in fine engraving and had it done for me.

The last time I wound the watch, I wound it too tight and it stopped. I took it back to Barry and Rachel in October 2020. Once again, he found parts, replaced them, and cleaned the watch. As I write this, it is restored and in the mail to me. When my daughter comes home to visit in March, I will give it to her. I'll give her the mismatched pair of cufflinks too, even though "they're not worth anything."

CHAPTER 8

RANTS AND RAVES

I was going to call this chapter *"Things I don't understand well and shouldn't be commenting on, but I insist on talking about them anyway,"* but the title was too long. Whether you agree or disagree with the comments herein, I hope you find some that provoke thought, or at least a smile or two.

DOING
LAUNDRY

Unless you are affluent, you can't afford to throw your clothes away and buy new ones once they are soiled. In most cases, you will want to wash even the new ones before you wear them. If you have to use a public laundromat, I offer my sympathy but no advice other than take a good book, as well as ear and nose plugs. I had to use a laundromat years ago and it was always the worst hours of my week. So, if you have to do laundry, a thankless mind-numbing job, try to simplify it.

I don't mind doing it now. I have the right equipment at home and have learned a few tricks. I fill up the washer, go back to my writing, wait for the buzzer, then throw it in the dryer, and go back to my writing again. With some people, it will be reading, watching TV, or cooking. The machines do all the work. You have only to react to audible signals.

Here are some tips to make the job easier.

1. Do not sort colours. Throw everything in one load. Buy all your new clothing in patternless grey shades. As you mix in the reds, blues, and whites which you already own, everything will soon become a pleasant darker grey. This will make mating socks and putting together outfits that match so much easier.

2. Wash everything in cold water. It will save you the money that you pay for the energy it takes to heat that water. I find no difference in the cleaning ability of cold or hot water. Do you think your grandmother had hot water when she beat her clothing on the rocks down by the creek?

3. Use the cheapest detergent; whether it is specified for hot or cold water makes no difference. Detergent makers create so many versions simply to get more shelf facings. Your grandmother used soap which she made from wood ashes, animal fat, and lye. If you run out of laundry detergent, use dish detergent. If you run out of that, grate up a bar of soap, or use a low perfume shampoo. It all works.

4. Buy all your clothing several sizes too big, then wash them once in hot water, and dry them on high heat. No matter what you do, most of it will shrink anyway. Pre-shrunk? They lie.

5. If you eventually tire of wearing all grey, go buy a bright red sweater. Make sure it is the cheapest one you can find and if the label says "colourfast," don't worry. They lie. What they really mean is that the colours will leach out faster than the cars run at Daytona. Toss it in with your greys and everything will come out with a nice pink highlight.

6. Do your wife's clothes separately, if you want to stay married.

WHY DON'T SONGBIRDS TRUST US?

Most of them disappear in the fall, as they migrate to warmer climes. From spring until that time arrives, however, they are all around us. We set out feeders for them, put up birdhouses that we have spent the winter building, look the other way when we see them building a nest—but they still don't trust us.

Robins are the worst of the bunch. We welcome them each spring when they return from the south. Many people mark on their calendar the day they see the first robin. But the minute robins see you moving in their direction, they fly away and hide.

How bad are the people where they spend their winters? Why do they not trust humans?

Some robins overwinter. You'd think that they would get closer to us then, seeking some kind of food. No, they retreat to the thickest forest, where they are protected from direct wind and snow, and eke out a bare existence from scratching through the forest floor litter.

There are exceptions. Some chickadees will get close—even take food from your hand—sometimes. My favourites, though, are the Canada jays, a.k.a. whisky jacks or grey jays. I see them in small groups, particularly in the fall and winter, occasionally accompanied by a blue jay.

They pass through quickly though, so when I see them, I immediately run into the house and back out with a slice of bread. I lean against the deck railing. When they see me waving the bread, they pitch on the opposite end of the rail. When I break off a small piece and hold it out, they do something remarkable.

The first bird runs along the rail and takes the offered bread and flies off with it. The next in line then runs up to my hand and takes the next piece—very orderly, civilized, and very Canadian. When that slice is gone, I'll go back inside for another, and as often as not they'll return and repeat the whole process.

If one was looking to capture a Canada jay, they could do it with their bare hand. But who would do that and alarm the whole group? So why don't small birds trust us? Geese are brave enough to chase us away. You can get quite close to seagulls and crows, and ducks will follow us around—but the smallest birds, by and large, don't trust us.

WORKING
WITH SO-CALLED
STUPID PEOPLE

Many of us are quick to characterize someone as lazy or stupid. Quite often, we revert to old sayings, using comparisons as verification of our belief. For example, "He's lazy as a cut cat" or "She's stunned as me arse." We speak of someone this way, and our listener laughs or adds another simile.

Stupid suggests someone of low intelligence. If that is indeed true, then we are as wrong in criticizing them as we would be in making fun of someone who is mentally ill or physically handicapped. They can do very little or nothing about their stupidity. Stupid has nothing to do with education, social, or economic status. If you are stupid, then you are simply stupid, in my opinion, without any need to show cause.

Often, though, someone is termed stupid because they are quiet, or offer no opinions, or simply lack self-confidence. Self-confidence can be built with proper support and guidance. When some so-called stupid people build their self-confidence, they open up and express opinions and have valuable ideas. These people are not stupid.

People who know what to do and how to do it but are too lazy to do it deserve no breaks, in my opinion. I would much rather be surrounded with truly stupid people, or those wrongfully termed as stupid, than lazy ones.

I knew a guy who told me that his father always said to him, "You're not very often right, but this time you are wrong." I suspect that such treatment, or even less blatant than that, in childhood, can stunt a person's self-confidence.

I have worked with the lazy, the stupid, the industrious, and the very bright in my career in sales and retail. The lazy ones I have no time for. I have never been able to successfully motivate a lazy person to do work. I don't believe that there is a cure for the condition. Like beating an addiction to alcohol or drugs, the desire to change has to start from within. Unfortunately, most of them are too lazy to try. Maybe I'm stupid to think so. Who knows?

THE REAL SMELL
of
POVERTY

I remember the smell of poverty—the actual *stink*. In a few of the places we lived, the house smelled of mildew. There were times my mother had only a galvanized washtub and homemade lye soap with which to do laundry. Without Javex or a similar product, it was hard to escape.

With six kids, she had to do laundry for eight of us, cook meals on a wood stove, do the dishes, keep the house clean, and mend and darn our clothing in her "spare" time. We had weekly baths in that galvanized tub too. The stink was from towels, towels that never completely dried between the youngsters' baths on Friday nights and on Saturdays, towels that picked up the mildew. The smell transfers to your skin.

You get used to that smell on your skin and you assume others smell the same. If I got close enough to someone and they were wearing perfume or aftershave, I assumed they were using it to hide their people smell. I'm not speaking of body odour. Body odour is different. I've smelled that too—as we all no doubt have. (Those aren't necessarily poor people. They may be without water that day, or careless, or lazy.)

Fortunately, times improved and we lived in houses with electricity and running water. I don't remember when or how I found out that the smell wasn't natural. By the time I was 12 and got to Grade 8, you probably couldn't smell me anymore. In Grade 8, I sat next to a girl who smelled like poverty. She was smart, she was kind, and she was funny, and I hung out a bit with her on weekends. I never said a word to her about it.

We'd meet in a neutral place, and go for walks, you know, just hang out. She wouldn't come to our house. She would never let me meet her at her place or walk her home. I knew where she lived, but I knew she didn't want me to know. I knew why.

She was clean but she was living way worse than we did when I was younger. She came from a large family, dirt poor—her dad was unable to work—and they lived in a house where you would not stable animals, let alone house people.

We moved away and I've not seen her since. Several times in my adulthood, I have smelled poverty again—as someone passed by or while I was standing in close lineups. I usually speak or smile, if they look friendly. I always think of Elaine. I hope that she is like that too and never forgets the stigma she must have felt from that stink of poverty: mildew.

IN DEFENCE
of
FENCES

There are many reasons for erecting a fence around your property:

1. To keep things in.
2. To keep things out.
3. To ensure privacy.
4. To hide things that you don't want to see.
5. To keep your neighbours out.
6. Because you like fences.

I put up an 8-foot fence on one side of my property for one of the above reasons. It worked well for a few years, until one winter the plough got too close and hit it. That broke some posts and cracked the cement in which others were anchored. I couldn't repair it in the winter, as the ground was frozen. Come spring, I realized that I couldn't remove the four cement blocks without a backhoe.

So I dug four new holes and cemented in four new posts. While it ruined the symmetry of a post every 8 feet, the finished job doesn't look too bad. But in the winter, before getting it fixed, I was worried that a heavy wind would blow the fence down on our parked cars. I decided to brace it, since a 24-foot section was already leaning forward at a 45-degree angle.

I was up on a 6-foot stepladder, my shoulder holding up that

24-foot section and working with a screw-gun, a hammer, and a crowbar, when a gust of wind took the fence and the ladder and my tools over on top of me.

But as I lay there, slowly regaining consciousness, and trying to disentangle myself, it felt like someone was watching me. I looked over and saw a ghostly figure in a long robe seemingly float toward me from the neighbouring property. All I could think of was, "I hope it's not the Grim Reaper or Jesus!" I was right, of course as it was just a curious but disinterested neighbour. He went back inside when he saw that I wasn't dead.

GOOD CALLS,
BAD CALLS,
and an
ETHICAL QUANDRY

Any salesman I've ever met can tell you stories about his/her worst calls—customers so obstinate that you could not reason with them. Rude or simply stupid people whom they hated to call on. No matter what you sell, or your territory, you're going to meet them.

Often, at night, when salespeople meet at hotels and get together for a coffee or a cold one, "bad calls" will be the topic of discussion. Long ago I would meet up with a group of salespeople in the same industry at a motel in PEI. The week's work done; we would catch the ferry back the next morning.

That night, however, we would get together and each of us describe our worst call that week. Then we'd vote whom we would award the title of "Ass**** of the Week." There was one particular dealer with a large office who had won so many of these awards that, had we provided plaques, his walls could not hold them all.

Then there are the good calls: Dealers who are patient, understand traffic tie-ups, late planes, or bad weather which may have prevented you, or your last order, from arriving on time. Dealers who offered you a coffee. Dealers who led with a kind word instead of a complaint. Dealers who didn't treat you as a nuisance—an interruption to their "perfect" day. Dealers who were loyal. Decent dealers.

These became your favourite calls. You went out of your way for them, and you'd bend any policy you could for them. Many became personal friends.

I had a favourite good call in one (undisclosed) territory. This dealer was honest to a fault, but my company wasn't so sure. With each weekly order, his store was claiming shortages, most often high-ticket items. The company flagged his account. After that, with every new order, each box was sealed at the warehouse only after two employees and the picker verified that the carton contained every item which was invoiced. They watched it being sealed. Then they watched as the whole order was loaded on the truck.

In order to rule out the truck driver as a suspect, his route was switched to another driver for a four-week period. He was not told why. Of course, we did not notify the dealer of these actions. The claims continued unabated.

The paperwork was sent to me, and I went in to review this problem with the dealer. He agreed that the shortages were outrageous. He asked me, "What is going on at the distribution centre? I don't know how many sales we've lost for product that didn't show up." Then I told him what we had been doing to monitor the problem and explained that claims had not increased at any other account.

Next, I told him, "Bill, I'd trust you with my life—but is it possible that you might have someone in your receiving department who is taking advantage of both of us?" He leaned back in his seat and said, "I can't believe it, but I'll find out today! Your truck arrives later this morning."

I contacted him later in the day. I won't give away details that could identify the dealer or staff member, but he told me that the receiver was confronted, readily confessed to theft, and was fired on the spot. The problem with shortages disappeared immediately.

Then came my quandary. The following day I went to visit a dealer in a close, but different, market area. When I walked in the door, here was the guy who had been fired the day before working in this other store! What should I do?

This dealer was not buying product from me, so I had nothing to lose or gain. Should I advise the owner so that he and his suppliers didn't risk similar losses? Should I speak to the employee, himself, about what happened the previous day, or should I say nothing? Perhaps the guy had learned his lesson, was regretful, and would become a better man. Would my interference kill his rehabilitation?

If I alerted the dealer to the possible danger, it might have brought him closer to buying from me. If I warned him, it might save him grief down the road. I chose to say nothing. I left the territory shortly after that for another job. Did I make the right choice? I've thought about it many times but I still don't know.

I DON'T KNOW
or
I'M NOT SURE?

It's the little things that annoy most of us, *not* the big things—like the government stealing our hard-earned money and spending it on their friends. Not the promises that politicians make and never keep. We expect those things. Here's one that bothers me.

It's mostly young people that say "I'm not sure." For example, you might ask, "How do I get to the nearest Tim Horton's from here?" They'll either give you directions or say, "I'm not sure." They will rarely say "I don't know." Why does no one want to admit that they don't know something which is so unimportant?

"I'm not sure " implies that you *think* you know but you are not *absolutely* certain. That's close enough. Tell me what you believe to be true. If you are wrong, I'll keep going and ask someone else. If you do not know, say so.

Suppose you stop beside the highway in Kentville, Nova Scotia, and ask someone, "If I keep on Highway #2 here, will I get to New Brunswick?" "I'm not sure" means you may end up in North Sydney and get lost in the fog, or you might cross a very long bridge and end up on PEI, but if in about two or three hours you see a sign that says "New Brunswick Border," then you are going the right way. The proper answers are "Yes," "No," or "I don't know."

If you ask your doctor if you have a broken leg, do you want him to say, "I'm not sure, but take these pills and walk carefully?" You want him to say "Yes," "No," or "I don't know—but I will find out."

All I want is a Tim Horton's and a small with cream and sweetener. I think there might be one in the next few blocks, but now I don't know. It's been 20 miles since he said, "I'm not sure but I think there's one just down the road."

IS RAISING
MINIMUM WAGE
THE ANSWER?

Some will likely call me a communist, a socialist, an idiot, or whatever else pops in their mind. I think the economic system is broken, deeply flawed, and was never fair to all people. The cause of disparity comes down to simple greed, in my mind.

All companies manufacturing or selling a product or providing a service can be forced by law to pay a predetermined minimum wage to their employees. That's where the trouble begins! If you raise the newest, untrained worker's compensation from $12 to $15 an hour, what do you do for the loyal, dependable employee who has been with you five years and is only now making $15?

You must compensate them higher, and then their supervisors, and then the department managers etc. No company that I know of will penalize their president or top management by cutting off their big bonuses to make up for the extra expense. And no company that I know of will settle for losing money, or merely breaking even to handle the added wage costs.

Then, after wages are raised, all these companies will raise their prices to pay for it. Goods and services will become that much more expensive for everyone. It isn't long before you're back where you started. The problem isn't simply that you make too little money. The problem is you can't buy enough with what you have. How do you fix that?

Start at the other end—the top! Establish maximum wages for CEOs, based on company size. Establish maximum wages for all positions and all government workers. Establish maximum profit levels for corporations, beyond which profits are taxed at 100 per cent. When CEOs can no longer afford a $3 million yacht, they will buy a $1 million one. When lower managers cannot afford a $100,000 speedboat, they will buy a $50,000 one.

Manufacturers won't make what they can't sell and most new mansions will become much smaller and less expensive and the bungalow and the car will become more affordable to lower income people. When you can just raise the price of everything to feed the rich, then the poor working person will always suffer.

What about the cost increases of raw materials to manufacturers, you say? Most of these increases are artificial. They are driven by greed—the desire to show higher profits and thereby lure more investors to their company. It is a rare raw material that gets so scarce that it truly becomes more valuable.

The only way to drive *down* the costs of consumer goods would be to implement this top-down system in the whole marketplace. Good luck with that! Suppliers of raw materials and consumer goods and services have to compete with foreign companies who use slave labour or employ workers at starvation wages.

Governments, both here and in other developed countries, let the cat out of the bag when they allowed imports of cheap consumer goods from China and other countries, with no concern for fair wages, worker safety, and employee benefits.

Companies like Wal-Mart took full advantage, and by so

doing were responsible for a multitude of factories closing, factories where their customers used to work,

What about part-time workers? When I started in retail in 1964, most workers in my industry (the grocery business) were full-time. Most employees worked Monday to Friday and had weekends off. The part-timers took over on weekends. They were mostly students—off from school, making spending money or saving for college.

The rest were mature women and men, starting as a part-time worker, and waiting for an opening to occur in order to become full-time workers.

Then, somewhere along the way, a few big corporations started the switch to hiring more part-time employees as their full-time ones left or retired. "Scheduling flexibility," they claimed. The real reason, though, was that you could pay part-time employees less per hour and did not have to provide the benefits—like sick days, health plans, and pensions.

Now many retail stores have most of their work done by part-time staff—who have to work two or three part-time jobs to put food on their table—and still have no benefits. How do you fix that? That one is easy. Legislate the number of part-time staff you can have as a percentage of total employees.

Overall, our economy is flawed and not easily fixed, and the rich and powerful do not want to see it fixed. To me, inflation is simply the result of greed. Having part-time staff is greed personified. Greed seems to be a universal human flaw.

IF MEN
HAD TO DO ALL
THE COOKING

Imagine that humans had evolved differently and the women all went out to work and all the men stayed home and did all the housework, including the cooking. Now I know, in most households today, both partners go out to work—and some share the duties at home. However, in most households today, the women still do most of the cooking.

If men had to do all the cooking, you would be able to buy peeled potatoes, carrots, and turnips in every grocery store! Instead of metal cans, women working in the food industry would invent microwavable packaging for soups and stews—pre-diluted—with pull tab tops. Cereal would be packed in small disposable bowls with plastic spoons.

Bread would come from the store, not only pre-sliced, but pre-buttered. Hot dogs and hot dog buns would have the same number of units in their respective packaging. Now you buy hot dogs 10 to a pack, but the buns are packed in eights. So that there isn't any waste, you need to buy four packs of hot dogs and five packs of buns to get it to even out. You put them all in the freezer, and once a year, discard the freezer-burned remainder.

We'd make changes in the grocery stores too. The bacon and eggs would be side by side in the refrigerated section. The breads and the spreads, like peanut butter and jam, would be together as well. In the meat counter next to the steaks would be barbecue sauces and steak spice. They call that cross merchandising and most men would be happy to find enough to make a meal without having to walk 5 miles.

POWER
TOOLS

Our house in Seal Cove was up for sale, as we decided to move to New Brunswick, where I had an attractive job offer. A young couple had viewed the house a few hours earlier, and we went out to leave them alone with the real estate agent. We were just back when a car pulled in the yard. It was the husband who had been there earlier, alone this time, wanting to look at the garage.

"I'm thinking of opening up a workshop," he said, "and just wanted to make sure there was room enough, and sufficient electrical outlets for the power tools that I'm planning on buying."

I didn't like doing this without the real estate agent present, but I thought, well, he's here. I didn't want to offend him and lose a possible sale. (But why he didn't want to look at it when he was there before, I couldn't figure out. Perhaps his wife was on a need-to-know basis about his future plans.)

He was amazed at all the outlets and the variety of power tools we had—including a table saw, bandsaw, router, jigsaw, sander, and a few more items.

"Wow," he said, "you wouldn't consider selling these to me, would you?"

"I'll have to ask my wife," I replied.

"Your wife," he responded with a derisive laugh. "You have to ask your wife?"

"Of course," I replied. "They're hers. I wouldn't even know how to turn some of them on."

His eyes widened. Without apologizing for his faux pas, he decided to go ahead and tell me his theory on where women should be spending their time. Fortunately, for him, my wife was not with us. Had she been, the little spitfire would have backed him over to the router and, when he was seated properly on it, turned it on to demonstrate its efficiency.

When I told my wife later what had transpired, she said, "I don't want to sell them and if I did, it wouldn't be to an arsehole like that!" They didn't buy the place, so I suspect that his wife may have had a little more say on where they were going to live than what he let on. Poor woman. I hope that in her new home she got some of the features that *she* wanted—along with her own private bedroom.